*Law*Basics

CONSTITUTIONAL LAW

Available soon:

Other titles in this Series

Agency
Delict
Evidence

*Law*Basics

CONSTITUTIONAL LAW

By

Jane Convery

Lecturer in Law, University of Edinburgh

EDINBURGH
W. GREEN/Sweet & Maxwell
1998

First published 1998

Published in 1998 by W. Green & Son Limited of
21 Alva Street,
Edinburgh, EH2 4PS

Typeset by Trinity Typesetting,
Edinburgh

Printed in Great Britain by Redwood Books,
Trowbridge, Wiltshire

No natural forests were destroyed to make this product; only farmed timber was
used and replanted

A CIP catalogue record of this book is available from the British Library

ISBN 0 414 01238 0

TABLE OF CONTENTS

TABLE OF CASES

1. THE UNITED KINGDOM CONSTITUTION

INTRODUCTION

As the term "the United Kingdom constitution" implies, constitutions and constitutional law are linked in a strong sense to the state. But constitutional lawyers must recognise the dimensions of constitutional law that exist beyond the state, *e.g.* European Community law and aspects of international law, and those which obtain at a sub-state level, *e.g.* devolution. Perhaps more than most, Scots lawyers are aware of these different dimensions as a result of the distinctive system of Scots law, and the changes which the establishment of a Scottish Parliament in 1999–2000 will bring.

At one level, constitutional law is about institutions—Parliament, government, the courts—and their powers and functions, and the relationships between them. At another level, it is about the relationship between the state and individual citizens, in particular the rights and liberties of the individual as against the state. Many constitutional systems provide the rules defining and regulating these subjects in a written document or documents. The United Kingdom constitution does not. British constitutional law consists of a diverse collection of rules and practices including statutes and case law, political practice and the procedures established by different institutions of the state to regulate their own tasks, *e.g.* the law and custom of Parliament.

As such, constitutional law is a vast and complex subject, confined not merely to legislation and cases but extending to legal and political theory, history, and modern political science. The aim of this book is not to cover the whole field of constitutional law, but to provide a basic guide to some of the more important aspects of the subject in a way which illustrates its diversity without overwhelming, or depressing, those who are trying to make sense of it. The book is no substitute for wider reading, but if it helps to orientate students as they embark on further study and enables them to identify the key issues, it will have done what it set out to do.

SOURCES OF CONSTITUTIONAL LAW

Legislation

Many Acts of Parliament have special constitutional significance, although it may be said for present purposes that such statutes do not enjoy a higher legal status as a consequence. Some examples will suffice. The Claim of Right 1689 of the Scottish Parliament and the Bill of Rights 1688 of the English Parliament contained the terms on which the thrones of James VII of Scotland and II of England, vacated following the Glorious Revolution of 1688, were offered to William and Mary: these statutes laid the foundations of the modern constitution by establishing parliamentary supremacy and firmly rejecting the claims of the Stuart kings to rule by prerogative right. By the Acts of Union, the Scottish and English Parliaments dissolved themselves in order to unite as one in 1707. Since the Union, statutes of constitutional importance include the Reform Act 1832, which laid the foundations of today's democratic franchise (see now the Representation of the People Act 1983); the Parliament Acts of 1911 and 1949, which made it possible to dispense with the consent of the House of Lords in the enactment of Acts of Parliament; and the European Communities Act 1972, which incorporated E.C. law into the legal systems of the United Kingdom.

Judicial decisions
The judges expound and apply the common law in their decisions in particular cases. Through the mouthpiece of the common law, the courts have provided authoritative (because binding on lower courts by the doctrine of precedent) clarification on a number of areas of constitutional significance, *e.g.* the existence and extent of prerogative powers claimed by the Crown; the legality of governmental acts and the remedies available to citizens injured by illegal acts; and indeed the existence and nature of the fundamental principle of the United Kingdom constitution, parliamentary supremacy.

Bear in mind three points:

- The common law is subordinate to statute law, so judicial decisions may be overturned or amended by Act of Parliament.
- E.C. law overrides the common law, and indeed Acts of Parliament.
- The European Court of Human Rights may hold that national judicial decisions are incompatible with the European Convention on Human Rights. If so, the United Kingdom comes under an international legal obligation to amend national law so as to achieve consistency with the Convention. At present, the Convention forms no part of domestic law, so that the courts cannot apply and enforce it directly. But the role of national courts in the protection of human rights will change with the incorporation of the Convention in 1998.

There are still areas of the law governed solely by the common law, but today the intervention of statutes means that the role of the courts is less creative than interpretive. However, the function of interpreting statutes is constitutionally important too. It is by no means a mechanical and self-executing task, and it has been said that the courts may even "supply the omission of the legislature" where this is necessary. A recent illustration of this occurred in *R. v. Home Secretary, ex parte Fayed* (1997), an application for judicial review of the Home Secretary's refusal of an application for citizenship. The court quashed the refusal, holding that even though the British Nationality Act 1981 expressly exempted the Home Secretary from giving reasons for his decisions, he was nevertheless under a duty to act fairly in the exercise of statutory discretions and that duty might extend to giving reasons.

Constitutional conventions

In *The Law of the Constitution*, Dicey spoke of "conventions, under-standings, habits or practices which, though they may regulate the conduct of the several members of the sovereign power ... are not in reality laws at all since they are not enforced by the courts."

This refers to the many rules of constitutional behaviour which are found in neither statutes nor judicial decisions but which are nonetheless observed by such constitutional actors as the Queen, the Prime Minister and Cabinet, M.P.s and judges. There is some dispute about whether these non-legal rules, or constitutional conventions, are *prescriptive* (saying what ought to happen) or merely *descriptive* (saying what does happen). Conventions are, at least, descriptive, because fundamentally they are rules of practice, founded on consistent patterns of constitutional behaviour. To take some examples:

- The Sovereign has, in strict legal terms, the power to refuse the Royal Assent to a Bill passed by the House of Commons and the House of Lords, but by convention the Sovereign must always give the Royal Assent on the advice of her ministers. Even when the Royal Assent was last refused—by Queen Anne, to the Scottish Militia Bill in 1708—it seems to have been done on ministerial advice.
- Convention also requires that the Queen exercise her power to appoint ministers on the advice of the Prime Minister, and that ministers should be drawn from Parliament.
- By convention, Her Majesty's government must have the confidence of the House of Commons. Thus when the government loses the confidence of a majority in the House of Commons—as Mr Callaghan's Labour government did on a motion of no-confidence in 1979—it must by convention resign.

To argue that a convention is prescriptive implies that what ought to be done, according to the convention, may be enforced. But there is no remedy for breach of a convention in the courts: *Att.-Gen. v. Jonathan Cape Ltd* (1976). This does not mean that the courts take no cognisance of conventions when deciding on questions of law, *e.g.* the courts may exercise only low-level control over executive action in areas traditionally subject to political control through the scrutiny of Parliament and the convention of ministerial responsibility: *Liversidge v. Anderson* (1942); *R. v. Environment Secretary, ex parte Nottinghamshire C.C.* (1986). But the courts cannot adjudicate on the existence and allegation of breach of a convention, simply because conventions are non-legal rules.

If the courts can provide no remedy, are there any sanctions for breach of a convention; and if not, why are they obeyed at all? It has been said that the reasons for obedience are positive and negative. In the positive sense, conventions are obeyed because they reflect prevailing constitutional values: it is appropriate that what a convention prescribes is done. In the negative sense, conventions are obeyed because political difficulties—even constitutional crises—may flow from disobedience.

However, it is well to be cautious when speaking of "breaches" of conventions. It would be difficult to draw up a list of conventions with which everyone would agree. The degree of obligatoriness of conventions is variable: at one end of the spectrum, there are those usages which have been observed for centuries and which are acknowledged as binding; at the other end, there are relatively new strands of constitutional practice which may or may not, in time, harden into rules. "Conventions are always emerging, crystallising and dissolving, and it is sometimes questionable whether a convention has been broken or has simply changed" (Turpin, 1995).

Thus the term "breach" may be apposite in the case of well-established conventions, such as that which requires that the Queen should always act on the advice of her ministers. But even here, there may be exceptional circumstances where it might not be unconstitutional for the Queen to act without, or in the face of, ministerial advice. In other cases, bear in mind that conventions are essentially rules of practice, and it is a virtue of conventions that they may evolve as practice adjusts to meet new circumstances and changing constitutional values. For example, the traditional convention of ministerial responsibility to Parliament, whereby ministers must accept responsibility for all that takes place within their departments and resign in the event of mistakes or maladministration, may well have altered in the light of contemporary constitutional practice. Moreover, many apparently consistent lines of practice may not assume the character of conventions at all: it was not suggested that hereditary peerages should no longer, by convention, be created when, in 1983, on the recommendation of Mrs Thatcher, hereditary peerages were conferred for the first time in over 20 years.

Due to the lack of clarity which can surround conventions, it might be argued that they should be codified or enacted as legal rules. There are a number of problems with this argument. First, codification would be fraught with difficulty. That in itself might not matter if the overall exercise were worth it. But, secondly, even written constitutions cannot provide for every possible eventuality in the form of legal rules. Codifying conventions would not remove the "penumbra of doubt" which surrounds all rules, legal or non-legal: the need would remain for certain usages and understandings to guide constitutional actors in their interpretation and application of the rules. Thirdly, the very nature of conventions as rules founded on consistent constitutional practice allows for the gradual evolution of the constitutional order as adaptation is necessary, without the need for new legislation or constitutional amendment. One might be suspicious of the degree of flexibility which flows from our reliance on conventions, but it is a fact that all constitutional systems must permit some elasticity if they are to be workable.

Other sources

We have noted the principal sources of constitutional law, but there are others which should be mentioned for completeness. The law and custom of Parliament is one. Parliament's exclusive authority over its own procedures, composition and internal affairs was asserted in the Bill of Rights 1689. The standing orders of the House of Commons, resolutions of the House, rulings of the Speaker and other aspects of parliamentary practice are the source of a number of important constitutional rules and understandings.

Scots law also regards the statements of the institutional writers, such as Stair, Erskine and Hume, as authoritative sources of law in the absence of subsequent contrary authority. English law does not treat legal literature as authoritative as such, but the influence of certain textbooks, *e.g.* Dicey's *The Law of the Constitution* and Erskine May's *Parliamentary Practice*, should not be underestimated.

Having looked at the sources of constitutional law and gained some idea of the nature of the subject, we move on next to the main institutions of the United Kingdom constitution: Parliament, central government and the courts. There is already a Scottish dimension to each of these institutions, but the nature of the government of Scotland will change at the turn of the century when the Scottish Parliament meets for the first time, and in Chapter 5 we discuss devolution and the background to it. It is also necessary to consider the principles of constitutional government which presently form part of British constitutional law and will continue to do so, at least for the time being: parliamentary supremacy, the rule of law and the separation of powers. We then look at constitutional law not from the viewpoint of institutions but from the viewpoint of the individual citizen and his or her relationship with the state. An important aspect of this is the European Convention on Human Rights, which is to be incorporated into domestic law in 1998. At a domestic level, the final chapters focus on the powers of the police, the law relating to freedom of assembly and public order, and judicial review of administrative action.

---

2. PARLIAMENT

THE MEETING OF PARLIAMENT

The meeting of Parliament involves the exercise of prerogative power as qualified by statute and convention. Parliament is summoned and dissolved by royal proclamation; it is also the Sovereign who prorogues Parliament, *i.e.* brings each annual session to an end. But the Sovereign cannot exercise these powers at will. In response to the efforts of the Stuart kings to do so, Article 13 of the Bill of Rights 1688 provided that "Parliament ought to be held frequently". In fact, Parliament has met annually since 1689. The Parliament Act 1911 provides that no Parliament shall last for more than five years, which period begins to run on the date appointed for Parliament to meet after a general election.

THE COMPOSITION OF PARLIAMENT

The Sovereign
We have noted the role of the Sovereign in summoning, proroguing and dissolving Parliament. The Queen is also a part of Parliament, in a formal sense, in that strictly speaking Acts of Parliament are Acts of the Queen in Parliament: bills approved by the House of Commons and House of Lords must receive the Royal Assent in order to become law (although by convention the Sovereign never refuses the Royal Assent).

The House of Lords
The House of Lords comprises Lords Spiritual (26 archbishops and bishops of the Church of England) and Lords Temporal. The Lords Temporal fall into the following categories: hereditary peers and peeresses; life peers; and Lords of Appeal in Ordinary. In total, the House of Lords has some 1,200 members.

There are some 800 hereditary peers and peeresses in their own right. Peeresses were barred from sitting in the past: the right of a peeress in her own right to take her seat in the Lords was established by section 6 of the Peerage Act 1963 (although it is of little significance as most hereditary peerages only descend through the male line).

An hereditary peerage cannot be renounced. In *Re Parliamentary Election for Bristol South East* (1964), Viscount Stansgate (better known now as Tony Benn) sought unsuccessfully to challenge the disqualification of members of the House of Lords from standing for election to the House of Commons. However, the case led to the enactment of the Peerage Act 1963, which allows hereditary peers to disclaim their titles for life. Disclaimer does not extinguish the peerage, and the succession of the heir is unaffected. If a member of the House of Commons succeeds to a peerage, he has one month from the death of his predecessor to disclaim, during which time he may not sit or vote in the Commons. If the death occurs during an election campaign, the new peer has one month from the declaration of the result to disclaim. The Act also gave existing peers the opportunity to disclaim within 12 months of the date on which the Act received the Royal Assent—July 31, 1963. This was fortuitous for the Fourteenth Earl of Home, who was appointed Prime Minister when Mr Macmillan resigned in October 1963. Lord Home disclaimed his peerage and was rapidly elected to the Commons in a by-election as Sir Alec Douglas-Home.

The Life Peerages Act 1958 provided that the Queen might confer life peerages on men and women with the right to sit in the Lords. There are currently just over 400 life peers, of whom one-fifth are female. Often appointed in recognition of political service or of reputation in particular walks of life, it is mainly life peers who constitute the "working House".

The conferment of life peerages on those appointed to judicial office in the House of Lords was also authorised by statute: Appellate Jurisdiction Act 1876, s. 6. Section 1 of the Administration of Justice Act 1973 provides that the maximum number of Lords of Appeal in Ordinary shall be 11, of whom, by convention, at least two are Scottish.

The House of Commons

There are currently 659 elected M.P.s, of whom 72 represent Scottish constituencies. The composition of the Commons is the consequence of the electoral system currently in use for parliamentary elections in the United Kingdom, namely the relative majority or "first past the post" system whereby the candidate who receives the most votes in a constituency— even if it is only one more than the runner-up—is elected to the seat. There is now a distinct shift in favour of more proportional electoral systems in many quarters. The Liberal Democrats have long been in favour of an electoral system based on proportional representation, and the principle has also received qualified support from Labour. Proportional representation is already used in Northern Ireland for elections to the European Parliament, and the present government is considering the introduction of proportional representation for European elections throughout the United Kingdom. Elections to the Scottish Parliament and Welsh Assembly in 1999 will be based on a combined system of first past the post and proportional representation.

There are a number of categories of disqualification from membership of the Commons. Although citizens of Commonwealth countries and the Republic of Ireland are eligible for membership, other foreign nationals are not. Other disqualified persons include those under the age of 21; mental patients; bankrupts; peers; clergymen of the Church of England and protestant Church of Ireland, ministers of the Church of Scotland and Roman Catholic priests. Since 1981, criminal convictions carrying a custodial sentence of more than one year disqualify: if the individual concerned is an M.P. at the time of conviction and sentence, his or her seat will be vacated.

The House of Commons Disqualification Act 1975 further excludes the holders of judicial office, civil servants, members of the regular armed forces, police officers, members of the legislature of any country or territory outside the Commonwealth, and holders of various offices on public boards and authorities. Acceptance of an office of profit under the Crown also disqualifies: it is this which provides the only mechanism available to an M.P. who wishes to "resign" his seat. The M.P. may request the Chancellor of the Exchequer to appoint him to the office of Steward or Bailiff of the Chiltern Hundreds or the Manor of Northstead. On appointment, his seat is declared vacant and a by-election is held to elect a successor.

THE FUNCTIONS OF PARLIAMENT

Providing and sustaining a government

In the United Kingdom we have a parliamentary executive: the government is drawn from, and is responsible to, Parliament. The Sovereign is bound by convention to appoint as Prime Minister the person who appears best able to command the confidence of the Commons, and to invite that person to form a government. As a rule, that person is the leader of the party having an overall majority of seats in the Commons. It is the endorsement of the elected members of the Commons which confers democratic legitimacy on the government and its legislation. Therefore, when it appears that the government has lost the confidence of the Commons (usually on a motion of confidence), convention obliges the government to resign. Note, however, that in modern constitutional practice, defeat in a vote on a government bill is not taken to signify loss of confidence in the government unless the bill is of a sort which is still treated as a matter of confidence by convention (*e.g.* the annual Finance Bills) or unless the government expressly states that the vote is to be treated as a matter of confidence.

This does not mean that a government cannot be formed unless one party secures an overall majority of seats (and indeed, from time to time, government majorities may be dispensed with, as where private members' bills are left to a free vote; and on issues of privilege). But a minority government is always in a precarious position, and it is unlikely to be long before a general election is advised or forced; *e.g.* having taken office as a minority Prime Minister in February 1974, Mr Wilson called a second election in October 1974. A minority government may forestall the inevitable loss of confidence for a time by entering into agreements with other parties, *e.g.* the "Lib-Lab Pact" of 1977–78 which sustained Mr Callaghan's minority administration. However, such arrangements have always proved to be unstable.

Some find repugnant the fact that M.P.s tend to place party loyalty (a loyalty firmly reinforced by the Whip system) above their role as parliamentarians. It is unsurprising, however, that this is the case, and it is pointless to suggest reforms which no government will introduce, *e.g.* secret voting instead of the present system of voting by walking through the division lobbies. The current position is to a great extent the product of the electoral system—by and large, a two-horse race which tends to produce majority governments of one stripe or another and therefore emphasises the importance of party cohesion.

Legislation

Parliament is the primary legislative institution in the United Kingdom and Acts of Parliament are the highest form of law. The enactment of an Act of Parliament begins with the laying of a bill before one of the two Houses of Parliament. The bill then undergoes a process of scrutiny in both Houses, at the end of which Commons and Lords must agree on the final text (although it is possible for the Commons to dispense with the agreement of the Lords in certain circumstances). The bill then receives the Royal Assent and thus becomes an Act of Parliament.

Bills fall into two categories: *private bills* and *public bills*. Erskine May defines private bills as "bills of a special kind, for conferring particular powers or benefits on any person or body of persons ... in excess of or in conflict with the general law." They have been used with greater frequency in recent years, notably by developers as a means of bypassing ordinary planning law. Private bills are introduced in Parliament by parliamentary agents acting on behalf of the prospective beneficiary of the legislation. After their second reading in each House, they are considered by a select committee, which considers whether the special powers sought are in order and in line with precedent. Any objectors to the bill are entitled to be heard by the committee before it decides whether or not to accept it.

Public bills are far more important. They relate to matters of general public interest and are introduced either by an M.P. or a peer. All government legislation is enacted by means of public bills. *Government bills* are sponsored by a minister and occupy the greater part of parliamentary time each session. *Private members' bills*, whereby backbench M.P.s may propose legislation, undergo the same procedure as government bills but are likely to fail for lack of time unless supported by the government.

The first formal stage of the legislative process is the *first reading*, where the bill is announced to Parliament. At *second reading*, the bill is explained to the House in which it was introduced (usually the Commons) and it is debated. If the principles of the bill are opposed, a vote follows the debate, and if the bill is defeated (as is usual for private members' bills, but very rare for government bills) it proceeds no further.

The bill is then sent for detailed scrutiny by a *standing committee* of some 20 M.P.s selected to reflect the party balance in the House. Bills of special significance, *e.g.* the Finance Bills which implement the Budgets, may be examined by a *committee of the whole House*. It is open to committees to amend bills, although amendments on matters of substance, as opposed to technicalities, are unusual.

The *report stage* follows the completion of the committee's task, when the bill is "reported" to the House. Further amendments may be tabled for debate at the report stage, although usually few of these can be addressed in the time available. Bills considered by a committee of the whole House also have a report stage unless they are passed without amendment; in that case, they proceed directly to *third reading*.

At third reading, which is generally a pure formality and may not even conclude with a vote, the bill is debated in its final form. It then proceeds to the House of Lords. The procedure in the Lords is like that in the Commons, except that the committee stages are usually taken on the floor of the Lords; the Lords very rarely vote on any of the readings of a government bill, in deference to the fact that the Lords have no real right to reject a bill (although they have been known to do so); and there is no provision for foreclosing debate in the Lords. In the Commons, by contrast, where timetabling is more of a problem, an *allocation of time* or *guillotine* motion may be moved, debated and voted upon by the House. The effect of the guillotine is to fix the time available for the remaining stages of a bill, which considerably cuts down remaining opportunities for scrutiny.

If the Lords make no amendments to a bill, it is automatically submitted for the Royal Assent. If amendments have been made, the bill returns to the Commons, which may agree to the amendments; substitute amendments of its own; or reject the amendments outright. In the latter two cases, the bill is sent back to the Lords accompanied by the Commons' reasons. As a rule, the Lords will accept the decision of the Commons. Occasionally, however, they stand their ground. In most such cases compromise will eventually be reached, but, very exceptionally, the two Houses will fail to reach agreement on a final text within the parliamentary session. In that event, subject to the provisions of the Parliament Acts 1911 and 1949, the bill lapses. Under the Parliament Acts, the House of Lords has no power to amend or delay a bill certified by the Speaker to be a money bill. The Lords can delay any other public bill for one session, but it is open to the Commons to revive the bill in the next session, leapfrog the Lords and proceed directly to the Royal Assent. The Lords do, however, retain a power of veto over private bills, statutory instruments and bills to extend the life of Parliament beyond its current five-year term.

Although the legislative process occupies a great deal of parliamentary time, the effectiveness of parliamentary scrutiny of government legislation is limited. The smaller the majority enjoyed by a government, the more vulnerable are its legislative intentions to amendment if not outright defeat, but large majorities tend to be more typical. And when the government has the support of a substantial majority, there is much truth in the comment that "Parliament's role is one of registration and legitimation: it cloaks legislation agreed elsewhere with the form and force of law" (Adonis, 1993).

In response to the perceived deficiencies of parliamentary scrutiny, a Select Committee on Modernisation of the House of Commons was appointed in June 1997 to recommend "ways in which the procedure for examining legislative proposals can be improved". The Committee has recommended, *inter alia*, the programming of bills in advance in preference to the guillotine; pre-legislative examination of draft bills by an ad hoc select committee or joint select committee drawn from the Commons and the Lords, or by the appropriate departmental select committee; and the adoption of a procedure whereby government bills may be carried over from one parliamentary session to the next.

Scrutiny of the executive
To the extent that most of the legislative business of Parliament involves government legislation, the legislative process itself provides some scope for scrutiny of the executive. But such scrutiny goes further than this (and is, perhaps, no more effective than in the context of legislation).

The government is responsible to Parliament for its acts and decisions, and a number of procedural mechanisms exist to facilitate and enforce this responsibility. *Parliamentary questions* take place every day when the Commons are sitting except Friday. Most answers given by ministers at these times are in response to earlier, written questions (and questions for written answer may be put at any time), but the M.P. concerned may raise oral supplementary questions based on the minister's reply.

Information may be withheld on a number of grounds. A minister may refuse to answer questions relating to matters for which he is not responsible. He may also refuse where the cost of retrieving the information would be excessive, or where it would be contrary to the public interest for the information to be disclosed. Undue reliance has been placed on these "escape clauses", and the 1996 report of the Scott Inquiry into the "Arms to Iraq" affair was deeply critical of the evasive, unhelpful and sometimes misleading answers ministers gave to questions. Note also that ministers, being in command of government information, have the advantage over M.P.s, whose ability to scrutinise effectively is hampered by the lack of information on which to base penetrating questions. A code of practice on "open government" has, however, been in place since 1994, with which ministers and civil servants are expected to comply in their parliamentary work. It may be that further improvements will flow from the enactment of a Freedom of Information Act, which has been promised by the present government.

Debates provide an alternative forum for scrutiny. *Adjournment debates* take place each day at the close of public business in the Commons, although they are unlikely to have much impact as ministers have advance notice of the subject of debate and time to prepare their defences. Members of Parliament may move for an adjournment of the House to permit a debate on an urgent issue, but *urgency debates* are rare. The Opposition has the opportunity to set the agenda for debates on *opposition days*.

The drawback of questions and debates is that, dominated by party loyalties and "adversary politics", they tend to collapse into political point-scoring. To an extent, the same problems are felt in select committees. Select committees have been a feature of parliamentary life for many years (*e.g.* the Public Accounts Committee, which reports to the Commons on its audits of departmental finances, was established in 1861). The present system of departmental select committees was established in 1979, when the new Conservative government implemented the proposals of the Select Committee on Procedure and reorganised the select committee structure to provide M.P.s with a regular and focused mechanism for scrutiny. Select committees are appointed for the life of each Parliament to examine the expenditure, administration and policy of the main departments and public bodies associated with those departments. Their membership reflects the party balance in the Commons: a majority of members will be backbench M.P.s from the government party. This can lead to voting along party lines when the committee decides upon the content of its reports.

Select committees have neither greatly altered the relationship between Parliament and government nor transformed an adversarial political culture into a more co-operative and consensual one. But they are an important addition to the machinery of state nonetheless: as the Select Committee on Procedure asserted in 1990, the new departmental select committees provided, in their first decade, "a far more vigorous, systematic and comprehensive scrutiny of ministers' actions and policies than anything which went before." But it is still fair to say that parliamentary scrutiny of the executive will continue to be a sporadic, low-intensity business unless and until the balance of power between Parliament and government is tilted somewhat away from the latter. The present situation is not only the fault of successive governments, anxious not to subtract from their power; M.P.s also have lacked the political will to pursue reforms or even to utilise more effectively the mechanisms for scrutiny which already exist.

PARLIAMENTARY PRIVILEGE

The privileges of Parliament are rooted in the law and custom of Parliament. At the opening of each new Parliament, the Speaker formally claims from the Crown for the Commons "their ancient rights and privileges", namely freedom of speech; freedom from arrest; the exclusive right to regulate composition;

and exclusive cognisance of internal affairs. Parliament also asserts an exclusive jurisdiction over the existence and extent of its privileges and over breaches of privileges, although this has provoked confrontation with the ordinary courts.

Freedom of speech
This is the most important privilege. Claims to freedom of speech were given a statutory foundation in Article 9 of the Bill of Rights 1688, which provided that "the freedom of speech and debates or proceedings in Parliament ought not to be impeached or questioned in any court or place out of Parliament."

Thus members may not be held liable, as a matter either of civil or criminal law, in respect of words spoken during debates or in the course of parliamentary proceedings (although members may fall foul of the disciplinary jurisdiction of the House itself). In 1938, for example, the privilege protected Mr Duncan Sandys M.P. from prosecution under the Official Secrets Act 1911 after he disclosed material concerning national security in a parliamentary question. The main effect of the privilege in civil law is the immunity it confers in the law of defamation. In *Church of Scientology v. Johnson-Smith* (1972), the Church brought a libel action against Mr Geoffrey Johnson-Smith M.P. in respect of comments he had made on television. It was held that Mr Johnson-Smith's speeches in the Commons were inadmissible as evidence of malice. Similarly, in *Prebble v. TV New Zealand* (1995), the Privy Council rejected TVNZ's argument that although Article 9 prevented parliamentary proceedings *founding* an action, it did not prevent them being used in support of an action or in its defence. Lord Browne-Wilkinson held that this argument was both inconsistent with authority and with the basic principle upon which the privilege rests—that, so far as possible, M.P.s should be able to speak freely without fear that what they say might later be used against them in court.

This does not mean that no reference whatsoever may be made in court to parliamentary proceedings. Since 1980, the House of Commons has permitted reference to be made in court to *Hansard* and published reports of committees. In *Pepper v. Hart* (1993), the House of Lords held that the courts might have resort to ministerial statements in *Hansard* if necessary to clarify ambiguities or to resolve apparent absurdities in legislation, stating that this would not involve "impeaching or questioning" freedom of speech. And an important amendment to Article 9 was made by section 13 of the Defamation Act 1996. This enables M.P.s to waive their privilege in order to pursue an action for defamation, and was utilised by Mr Neil Hamilton, ex-M.P. for Tatton and former minister for corporate affairs, in his action against *The Guardian* (although the action was withdrawn the day before the hearing was due to start).

The scope of the privilege is unclear owing to the inexact nature of the term "proceedings in Parliament". In 1938, the House of Commons asserted that the privilege extends to "everything said or done by a member in the exercise of his functions as a member in a committee in either House, as well as everything said or done in either House in the transaction of parliamentary business." Physical location does not provide a conclusive test: it was held in *Rivlin v. Bilainkin* (1953) that defamatory letters were not protected merely because they had been posted to M.P.s within the Palace of Westminster. By the same token, a "proceeding in Parliament" may take place outside, or nowhere near, Parliament, as the Committee of Privileges held in 1968 after a meeting of a sub-committee of the Select Committee on Education and Science at Essex University was disrupted by protestors.

A difficult case arose in 1958, when Mr George Strauss M.P. wrote a letter to the Paymaster-General criticising the practices of London Electricity Board. The letter was brought to the attention of the Board, which threatened to sue Mr Strauss for libel unless he retracted his remarks and apologised. Mr Strauss referred the matter to the Committee of Privileges, which found that the letter constituted a "proceeding in Parliament" within the meaning of Article 9. Subsequently, however, the Commons held on a free vote that the letter was not a proceeding in Parliament and that the Board had not, therefore, acted in breach of privilege.

If parliamentary proceedings are protected by Article 9, what of their publication outside Parliament? This question generated one of the great confrontations between Parliament and the courts in 1839 when, by order of the Commons, *Hansard* published a report stating that an indecent book published by Stockdale was circulating in Newgate Prison. Stockdale sued *Hansard* in defamation (*Stockdale v. Hansard* (1839)). The Commons ordered *Hansard* to plead the authority of the Commons and that the Commons had resolved the case to be one of privilege, which resolution could not be challenged by the courts as each House was the sole judge of its own privileges. The court rejected *Hansard*'s defence. It was held that mere resolutions of the House could not change the law, and that it was for the court to determine the existence and extent of parliamentary privileges when their assertion affected individuals outside Parliament. Here, privilege did not extend to permitting publication of defamatory material outside of Parliament.

The decision in *Stockdale v. Hansard* led to the enactment of the Parliamentary Papers Act 1840, which statutorily extends the protection of absolute privilege from civil or criminal proceedings to papers published under the authority of Parliament as certified by an officer of either House. Qualified privilege applies to publications of fair and accurate reports of parliamentary papers, so that there is no liability in defamation without proof of malice.

Freedom from arrest

This privilege protects members from civil arrest, but not from arrest in connection with criminal offences. Since the abolition of imprisonment for debt in the nineteenth century, the privilege has had little significance. However, it was held in *Stourton v. Stourton* (1963) that a member (in this case, a peer who had failed to comply with a maintenance order) is immune from committal for contempt of court where imprisonment is sought in order to enforce performance of a civil obligation. Collateral privileges flow from the basic principle underlying freedom from arrest, namely the right of Parliament to the uninterrupted attendance and services of its members, *e.g.* exemption from jury service.

Exclusive right to regulate composition
Formerly, the most important aspect of this privilege lay in the Commons' right to determine the result of disputed parliamentary elections. This jurisdiction has now been transferred by statute to the courts. The Houses of Parliament do, however, retain the right to determine whether a person is disqualified from membership of either House. Thus in 1960, the Commons declared vacant the seat of Mr Tony Benn M.P. when he succeeded to a viscountcy on the death of his father and barred him from the chamber. The Commons may also expel a member on grounds other than disqualification, *e.g.* the expulsion of Mr Garry Allighan M.P. in 1947 for gross contempt of the House.

Exclusive cognisance of internal affairs
Each House claims the exclusive right to control its own proceedings and to regulate its internal affairs without intereference from the courts. By and large, the courts have acquiesced in this privilege. It is one reason why the courts decline to investigate alleged procedural defects when the validity of an Act of Parliament is challenged (*Pickin v. British Railways Board* (1974)). Similarly, in *Bradlaugh v. Gossett* (1884), the court held that it had no jurisdiction to intervene when Mr Bradlaugh, an atheist who had been refused the opportunity of taking the oath required before an M.P. may sit and vote, contested the legality of a resolution of the House to exclude him and sought an injunction to restrain the Serjeant-at-Arms from enforcing that resolution.

Penal jurisdiction
The Houses of Parliament retain a jurisdiction to deal with breaches of privilege and contempts. "Contempt of Parliament" is an umbrella term for any offences punishable by the House, namely conduct which offends against the authority and dignity of the House, or, to quote Erskine May:

"any act or omission which obstructs or impedes either House in the performance of its functions, or which obstructs or impedes any member or officer of such House in the discharge of his duty, or which has a tendency, directly or indirectly, to produce such results."

"Contempt" therefore includes breaches of privilege, *i.e.* infringements of any of the specific privileges considered above. The distinction between the two may be important, however, for while the Houses cannot extend the scope of their own privileges, and questions of the existence and extent of privilege may be addressed by the courts, the list of possible contempts remains open and the courts cannot question the causes of committal for contempt. Thus in the *Case of the Sheriff of Middlesex* (1840), when two sheriffs sought to recover damages owed by *Hansard* after *Stockdale v. Hansard* (1839), the Commons committed Stockdale and the sheriffs for contempt. In habeas corpus proceedings to release them, it was held that the ordinary courts had no power but to accept the statement of the House that the committal was for contempt.

Established categories of contempt include disorderly conduct within the precincts of the House; obstruction of members going to or coming from the House; bribery, corruption and other species of dishonesty; and refusal to give evidence before committees of the House. Specific examples may be given. In 1963, Mr John Profumo M.P., the Secretary of State for War, was held to have committed contempt by falsely denying before the Commons any association with persons regarded as a security risk. More recently, the actions of a journalist who purported to offer M.P.s "cash for questions" were held contemptuous, even though a number of M.P.s accepted.

The fact that certain conduct is found to constitute contempt does not mean that the House will take further action against the contemnor. The Commons resolved in 1978 only to use its powers of punishment when "satisfied that to do so is essential to provide reasonable protection for the House, its members or its officers, from such improper obstruction or attempt or threat of obstruction as is causing or is liable to cause substantial interference with the performance of their respective functions." Nevertheless, the range of penalties at the theoretical disposal of the House is considerable. A member may be expelled or suspended; members or "strangers" may be admonished or reprimanded at the Bar of the House. Persons may be committed for contempt, without recourse to the ordinary courts; and the House retains a power, last used in 1880, of imprisonment (although it has no power to impose fines).

---

3. THE EXECUTIVE

INTRODUCTION

The functions of the state may be categorised as legislative, executive and judicial. The legislative function, vested primarily in the Queen in Parliament, involves the making of laws of general application and the conferment of delegated legislative powers on other bodies. The judicial function involves the settlement of disputes of fact and law by the courts and other bodies vested with judicial powers. The executive function, broadly speaking, is what is left. It ranges from matters of high policy such as defence and foreign relations through to the day-to-day administration of public services.

Historically, the executive was identified with the person of the monarch and executive power with the royal prerogative. The vast majority of executive powers today derive from statute, but the prerogative remains an important source of executive power in certain areas of government. Most prerogative powers today are exercised by or on the advice of ministers, who are responsible to Parliament for the way in which they exercise these powers or the advice that they give. By the same token, the constitutional battles of the seventeenth century between Crown and Parliament, culminating in the Glorious Revolution of 1688, settled that prerogative powers could be abolished, restricted or otherwise controlled by statute. Where a statute deals with the same subject-matter as a prerogative power, the former overrides the latter: *Att.-Gen. v. De Keyser's Royal Hotel* (1920). But *express* statutory words are needed if a prerogative power is to be abolished: as the House of Lords accepted in *Burmah Oil v. Lord Advocate* (1964), the statute will otherwise merely apply until repealed, but once repealed the prerogative power will revive.

A possible "third source" of executive power is derived from the fact that, as a matter of British constitutional law, all is allowed except that which is expressly prohibited by law. Thus, the absence of positive authority to act may nevertheless count as a "source" of executive power, provided no legal prohibition exists to stop such action: *Malone v. Metropolitan Police Commissioner* (1979).

THE SOVEREIGN

The Queen is Head of State. In strict legal terms, the prerogatives of the Crown are vested in her, and a few prerogative powers, *e.g.* the conferment of certain honours, remain personal to the monarch. Note, however, that in modern usage, "the Crown" is for practical purposes synonymous with "central government" (*Town Investments v. Department of the Environment* (1978)), and it is ministers of the Crown who exercise prerogative powers or advise on their exercise. Even the term "advise" is misleading because, by convention, the Sovereign's freedom of action is very limited.

Essentially, therefore, the executive role of the Sovereign is dignified rather than effective. Yet it has been said that "the Sovereign has, in a constitutional monarchy such as ours, three rights—the right to be consulted, the right to encourage and the right to warn" (Bagehot, 1867; Heseltine, 1986). Moreover, there may be circumstances in which the constitutional role of the Sovereign *could* assume an effective dimension.

Hung Parliaments and the prerogatives of appointment and dissolution
The Sovereign appoints a Prime Minister in an exercise of the prerogative. Modern politics, coupled with the constraints of convention, mean that the prerogative of appointment will fasten on the person who is best able to command the confidence of the Commons—the leader of the party having an overall majority of seats in the House. General elections usually produce such majorities. But in the event of a hung Parliament, what should happen may be less clear.

In the election of December 1923, the Prime Minister, Mr Baldwin, lost his overall majority in the Commons, although his was still the largest party. He continued in office and waited to meet Parliament, as he was entitled to do. Baldwin was then defeated in the vote on the King's Speech—a matter of confidence—and at that point resigned, because plainly he was unable to command the confidence of the Commons. The King appointed Mr MacDonald as Prime Minister. There was no fresh election and no need of one; and the choice of MacDonald involved no exercise of discretion on the King's part. It was dictated by the political circumstances: coalition under Baldwin being impossible, MacDonald was best placed to command the confidence of the Commons as the head of a minority government.

In the election of 1929, Mr Baldwin lost his majority again—and this time his party was no longer even the largest party in the Commons, although no other party had an overall majority either. Baldwin resigned immediately: the factors which had prevented him leading a coalition government or relying on support from other parties in 1923 were still present. Again, the King sent for Mr MacDonald, and again, no royal discretion was involved in that choice.

But the Prime Minister in this situation is not obliged to resign immediately. If the possibility of coalition exists, the Prime Minister may explore it. So in February 1974, Mr Heath did not resign until four days after the election, during which time he pursued—unsuccessfully—the prospect of a coalition Cabinet containing Liberal M.P.s. Labour was the largest party by five seats and was prepared to form a government with no help from other parties even though it lacked an overall majority. The Queen duly sent for Mr Wilson.

None of these hung Parliaments required recourse to the Sovereign in anything but a formal sense. But there are no rules to govern these situations, and the precedents themselves only provide guidance. Thus hung Parliaments *might* produce situations in which the Sovereign would have to act without, or even in the face of, ministerial advice. For example, a minority administration is formed but is shortly defeated on a motion of no-confidence; or a coalition government is formed but collapses within weeks of the election. The Prime Minister concludes that the newly-elected Parliament is unworkable, because incapable of sustaining a government in office, and advises the Queen to dissolve Parliament a second time so that a second election may be held. How should the Queen respond?

In 1951, the King's Private Secretary set out the principles governing (in his view) the Sovereign's right to refuse a second dissolution:

"The Sovereign could properly refuse a dissolution if satisfied that a) the existing Parliament was still vital, viable and capable of doing its job; b) a general election would be detrimental to the national economy; c) he could rely on finding another Prime Minister who could carry on his government for a reasonable period with a working majority."

Thus, had Mr Heath not resigned in 1974 but requested a second dissolution, the Queen would have been entitled to refuse because an alternative administration to Mr Heath's was available.

The position may differ, however, if the second dissolution is requested not by the Prime Minister who requested the first, but by his successor in a hung Parliament. In 1974, Mr Wilson assumed that a dissolution was his for the asking at any time, with or without defeat on a motion of confidence. In the volatile circumstances of 1974, he was probably right (and he did go to the country again in October 1974). But Mr Wilson might not have been right if, for example, the Conservatives and Liberals had managed in the meantime to agree on some form of coalition government, because then an administration could have been formed from the existing Parliament.

In short, any theory of "automatic dissolution" at the request of the Prime Minister must be regarded as misconceived. It is unlikely that the role of the Sovereign will be anything more than formal, even in cases of difficulty: there should be no reason to refuse a request for a dissolution and no need for royal discretion in the choice of Prime Minister. But the prerogatives of the Crown in this area provide a "safety valve" should it appear that politicians are abusing the system, and the fact that the powers exist may deter such abuse. Moreover, there are examples of exercise of the prerogatives in response to perceived abuse. In 1926, the minority Liberal Prime Minister in Canada requested a dissolution from the Sovereign's representative, the Governor-General. The Governor-General believed that the Conservative leader could form a government having majority support in the existing Parliament, and refused. The Prime Minister resigned and the Governor-General appointed the Conservative leader in his place. Days later, the new government was defeated on a motion of confidence, leading to the dissolution which had been denied to its Liberal predecessor. In the general election that followed, the Liberals were returned with a convincing majority. This illustrates that the Sovereign should not seek personally to exercise her legal powers in anything but extreme circumstances. But it does not prove that the personal exercise of the prerogatives of appointment and dissolution will always be unconstitutional.

The prerogative of dismissal
As the Sovereign's effective power to appoint a Prime Minister is reduced almost to nothing by convention, so too is the Sovereign's power to dismiss a Prime Minister. Indeed in *Adegbenro v. Akintola* (1964), Lord Radcliffe stated that the exercise of the "Sovereign's right of removal ... is not regarded as being within the scope of practical politics."

Yet the right of removal has been exercised in recent times. In 1975, Australia was governed by a Labour administration under Mr Whitlam, but the Opposition had a majority of seats in the Australian Senate. The Senate refused to pass money bills authorising government expenditure, which led to a rapid depletion in the funds available to maintain public services. Mr Whitlam requested the Governor-General to dissolve the Senate. The Governor-General was only prepared to grant a full dissolution so that there could be a general election. When Mr Whitlam refused to change his advice, the Governor-General dismissed him and his government and appointed Mr Fraser, the Opposition leader, in his place, on condition that he would guarantee supply and advise a dissolution and general election. In the event, Mr Fraser won the election.

Was this situation so extreme as to justify the exercise of the prerogative of dismissal? Arguably, the Sovereign should only exercise her prerogatives personally and without advice where necessary to safeguard the parliamentary and democratic basis of the constitution (*e.g.* where a government fails to seek a dissolution of Parliament after five years have expired since the last election). Beyond that, the legitimacy of the monarchy rests upon political neutrality on the part of the Sovereign, and the appearance of neutrality would be gravely undermined were the Sovereign to intervene in anything other than a constitutional crisis, where it is more or less clear that the "safety valve" must be pressed into service.

CENTRAL GOVERNMENT

The Prime Minister
The Prime Minister is a creature of constitutional convention. There is hardly any legal underpinning to the office and only cursory recognition of the office in statute. It is rare for statutes to confer powers on the Prime Minister: his powers flow, essentially, from the fact of being in charge, and so long as the Prime Minister retains the confidence of his Cabinet and party, these powers are extensive. For example, it is the Prime Minister who generally advises the Queen on the exercise of important prerogatives of the Crown, and it is the Prime Minister who controls the machinery of central government. These powers are reinforced by the convention of collective ministerial responsibility, whereby all government ministers are bound to defend and promote government policy, however that may be arrived at.

The Deputy Prime Minister
Formerly there was doubt as to the existence of this office. The objection was that, by nominating a deputy, the Prime Minister was pre-empting the royal prerogative of appointment by setting out a preferred line of succession. This must now be regarded as irrelevant. Labour governments have tended to include a Deputy Prime Minister to underscore the status of the elected deputy leader of the party. The deputy leadership of the Conservative party, by contrast, is in the gift of the leader, who may choose to appoint a Deputy Prime Minister. Certainly the Prime Minister is not bound to appoint a Deputy, but there are no longer any constitutional difficulties if he chooses to do so; and there may be good political and administrative reasons for the appointment.

Ministers of the Crown
Section 8(1) of the Ministers of the Crown Act 1975 defines a minister as "the holder of any office in Her Majesty's Government in the United Kingdom". Ministers are appointed to their office by the Queen on the advice of the Prime Minister.

We may distinguish between Cabinet ministers, usually designated Secretaries of State, who have overall responsibility for particular departments; departmental ministers of state, who share in the administration of a department and who may have specific portfolios (*e.g.* the Minister for

Defence Procurement and the Minister for the Armed Services within the Ministry of Defence); and parliamentary private secretaries and under-secretaries of state, who assist in a department's parliamentary work.

By convention, ministers must be members of the House of Commons or the House of Lords. The House of Commons Disqualification Act 1975, s. 2, provides that no more than 95 ministers may sit and vote in the Commons. Schedule 1 to the Ministerial and Other Salaries Act 1975 places limits on the total number of ministerial salaries payable at any one time. These provisions are practical limitations on the Prime Minister's power of patronage, but there is no legal limit on the number of ministers that the Crown may appoint, provided that the excess are members of the House of Lords and/or unpaid. Peers as ministers are a necessary consequence of the statutory provisions, and it is not uncommon for a political ally of the Prime Minister to be elevated to high office through the conferment of a life peerage.

Note also the Law Officers of the Crown. The Law Officers for Scotland are the Lord Advocate and the Solicitor-General, who may or may not be M.P.s (although it is customary to confer a life peerage on the Lord Advocate if he is not an M.P.). The Law Officers for England and Wales are the Attorney-General and the Solicitor-General: they are always drawn from the House of Commons.

The Cabinet

Like the Prime Minister, the Cabinet is a creature of convention—there are no legal rules governing its composition, functions or procedure, although the Ministerial and Other Salaries Act 1975 restricts the number of salaried Cabinet posts to 20, apart from the Prime Minister and Lord Chancellor.

The Cabinet emerged and developed in the late eighteenth century. In the nineteenth century, when government was relatively small, it was the engine-room of government; and it has been likened to the board of directors of a company. Collectively and in private, the Cabinet discussed and decided on government policy, resolved disputes between departments and provided general oversight and co-ordination. This traditional model of Cabinet government was bound together by conventions relating to the confidentiality of Cabinet discussions and collective responsibility for government policy. If a Cabinet minister felt unable to support agreed policy, convention required him to resign.

In the twentieth century, however, this traditional model has been undermined by overload. In 1963, Richard Crossman argued that the Cabinet had become a dignified rather than effective institution; and in 1983, the former Cabinet Secretary Lord Hunt said that "we are imposing more and more on a system of collective decision-taking that was designed for quite a different era." Government has grown immensely in volume, intensity and complexity, yet the Cabinet is still the same size and still meets only once a week. Efforts have been made to improve the capacity of the Cabinet to cope with modern demands, notably in establishing the Cabinet Office after the First World War; and, since the Second World War, in delegating much Cabinet business to Cabinet committees. Indeed today, *Questions of Procedure for Ministers*—the Cabinet rulebook—states that issues must be settled in committee as far as is possible; and successive Prime Ministers since the 1960s have made clear that matters should only be taken from committee to Cabinet if agreement is impossible and only then with the consent of the committee chairman.

These developments have contributed to the twentieth century dispersal of power away from Cabinet. From being the effective heart of the government machine in the nineteenth century, the Cabinet today considers few policy and legislative initiatives, and even those matters which are referred to Cabinet go there in most cases only for rubber-stamping rather than for proper consideration and collective commitment. As the traditional model of Cabinet government has come under strain, so the cement which held that model together—confidentiality and collective responsibility— has begun to crumble, as persistent "leaking" and crises such as the Westland Affair in 1986 illustrate.

A further consequence in the decline of traditional Cabinet government, some argue, is an increase in the powers of the Prime Minister. Crossman suggested that the institutional mechanisms and conventions which once served a collective, collegiate body had come to serve the Prime Minister instead. Thus the Cabinet Office was in reality the Prime Minister's Office; and collective responsibility, which had once meant the responsibility of a group of equal colleagues for decisions taken collectively, had come to mean "collective obedience to the will of the man at the apex of power." There is some truth in these views. But Mrs Thatcher's premiership, often taken as a shining example of "Prime Ministerial government", shows that however powerful the Prime Minister may be, that power is ultimately conditional upon the support of the Cabinet. This is true even when the government is supported by a healthy Commons majority, and truer still when its majority is fragile.

The civil service
The traditional civil service was the product of the Northcote-Trevelyan Report (1854), which established the civil service hallmarks of anonymity, political impartiality and selection on merit. It provided a source of stability and continuity, enabling administration to be carried on smoothly from one government to the next. In keeping with this tradition, the Head of the Home Civil Service stated in *The Duties and Responsibilities of Civil Servants in relation to Ministers* (1986) that "the executive powers of the Crown are exercised by and on the advice of Her Majesty's ministers, who are in turn answerable to Parliament. The civil service as such has no constitutional personality or responsibility separate from the duly elected government of the day." It follows that civil servants bear no political or public responsibility for departmental tasks, and to the extent that they may be exposed to public scrutiny—notably before departmental select committees—they are bound by the so-called Osmotherly Rules only to answer questions on the minister's behalf and not to answer questions about policy formulation.

The 1986 guidelines were criticised at the time as an outdated restatement of traditional constitutional doctrine. But the new civil service code which replaced the 1986 guidelines in 1996 emphasises, as before, the responsibility of civil servants as servants of the Crown. It does not in any concrete sense recognise that civil servants may owe duties—to Parliament, or to the public—other than their duty to the government of the day. In 1996, the Commons Public Services Committee debated whether civil servants should have either a right or a duty to expose wrongdoing, but reached no conclusions. Thus a civil servant who perceives maladministration or impropriety may only report the matter in accordance with internal departmental procedures: publicly exposing wrongdoing may attract either criminal or civil liability (*R. v. Ponting* (1985); *Att.-Gen. v. Guardian Newspapers (No. 2)* (1990)—the *Spycatcher* case).

Orthodox constitutional doctrine concerning the position and duties of civil servants has become even less convincing in the light of the fundamental reforms in the structure of the civil service which have taken place over the last decade. Stemming from concerns about the size, cost and inefficiency of the civil service, these reforms initially took the form of downsizing and pay restraints. But in 1988, the report *Improving Management in Government: The Next Steps* recommended the complete separation of policy-making functions from service-delivery functions. The latter, covering an estimated 95 per cent of civil service activity, would be devolved to *executive agencies* instead of being undertaken by traditional Whitehall departments. Departments were therefore required to review their activities and assess their suitability for hiving off to agencies. The rigour of the procedure intensified in 1991 with the introduction of "market testing". This requires departments to look at particular functions and ask whether that function can be abolished; if not, whether it can be privatised; if not, whether it can be contracted out to a private company; if not, whether it can be hived off to an agency. Only if the answer to all of these questions is "no" should things stay as they are.

Over 100 executive agencies have now been established and up to 40 more are in the pipeline. It is estimated that, as the 1988 report predicted, almost all civil servants will be working for agencies by the turn of the century. Each agency operates within the terms of a framework document, which sets out the respective responsibilities of the relevant minister and agency chief executive, performance targets (including strict financial targets and spending limits) and other operating arrangements. The chief executive answers to the minister for his agency's performance in implementing the policies settled by the minister; the minister, in turn, answers to Parliament for the agency's work—at least in theory.

Next Steps agencies are only one aspect of what is often termed "New Public Management" or the "marketisation" of the state. The dynamic behind the reforms is a belief that governmental efficiency can be improved by remodelling central government in a way which mimics the private sector and the efficient business practices and disciplines of the free market. Nor have the reforms taken place only on the "supply side". In a genuine market, consumers have a part to play. Thus the Citizen's Charter initiative was launched in 1991 to specify what the government's "customers" are entitled to expect from public services and to provide mechanisms for redress should those expectations be disappointed.

Efficiency in government is an important objective. But it is argued that efficiency cannot be measured in terms of cost-cutting alone and that this objective must be balanced against the objective of providing high-quality public services. Also, concern has been expressed that the "marketising" of the state has created a tension between old-fashioned administrative relationships based on the ethos of public service, and contractual or quasi-contractual relationships based on the profit motive and the pursuit of efficiency. Perhaps most importantly, the restructuring of the state has not been accompanied by a reassessment of the constitutional position of civil servants, or by effective avenues of accountability.

ACCOUNTABILITY

Accountability, an obligation resting on those who exercise power over others, has two aspects. The *explanatory* aspect involves justifying and explaining why certain policies were pursued and certain decisions taken. The *amendatory* aspect involves accepting blame when things go wrong and ensuring that mistakes are rectified. Accountability is important for two reasons. First, government is not infallible. Accountability should reduce the risks associated with governmental fallibility, for if government bodies feel obliged to justify their decisions and answer for their mistakes, they are more likely to think things through properly and avoid making mistakes in the first place. Secondly, although one may disagree with a government and its policies, it is easier to accept its decisions if one is confident that it takes care in making its decisions, that it acts in good faith and is willing to be held to account. Thus accountability is a form of "institutional morality" in a liberal democracy: it is conducive to cohesion.

According to traditional constitutional theory, the main avenue of accountability is political—the responsibility of ministers to Parliament for policy choices and the quality of administration. In keeping with this traditional view, civil servants bear no constitutional responsibility for departmental errors: the minister must answer for them. It is one of Parliament's key constitutional functions to scrutinise and check the executive, and to enforce ministers' obligations to explain and justify departmental acts and decisions. When a minister cannot satisfactorily account for something that took place within his department, then the Commons may withdraw its confidence from the minister on a motion of censure, forcing the minister to resign. The minister might pre-empt this by resigning anyway. Similarly, where the government as a whole comes under attack for its policies and loses the confidence of the Commons, the government collectively is obliged to resign. This doctrine is the basis of the traditional convention of ministerial responsibility.

There are some examples of resignations apparently in accordance with the convention, notably that of Sir Thomas Dugdale over the Crichel Down Affair in 1954, and, in 1982, those of the Foreign Secretary, Lord Carrington, and two Foreign Office ministers because of failure correctly to interpret

Argentine intentions prior to the Falklands War. But the great majority of ministerial resignations have less to do with proven incompetence or error than other factors, such as personal or financial scandal. It is therefore argued, rightly, that reliance on the convention of ministerial responsibility to Parliament as the primary mechanism of accountability is worthless, because the convention is no longer operative. This is partly because the Commons itself no longer works in a way which would enable it to withdraw its confidence from failing ministers:

"most charges never reach the stage of individualisation at all: they are stifled under the blanket of party solidarity. Whether a minister is forced to resign depends on three factors: on himself, his Prime Minister and his party. For a resignation to occur, all three factors have to be just so, the minister compliant, the Prime Minister firm, the party clamorous. This conjuncture is rare" (Finer, 1956).

But a convention which stipulates loss of office as a penalty seems unrealistic and unfair today; the growth of government means that individual ministers cannot be expected anymore to know about everything that takes place within their departments. Unless the minister is personally at fault, should he be expected to resign? After the Crichel Down Affair, the Home Secretary, Sir David Maxwell-Fyfe, appeared to suggest that he should not:

"In the case where there is an explicit order by a minister, the minister must protect the civil servant who has carried out the order. Equally, where a civil servant acts properly in accordance with the policy laid down by the minister, the minister must protect and defend him. Where an official makes a mistake ... but not on an important issue of policy ... the minister acknowledges the mistake and ... states that he will take corrective action within his department. [But] where action has been taken by a civil servant of which the minister disapproves and has no prior knowledge ... [he] is not bound to defend [the civil servant]."

There are indications that such an approach is taken in practice. Thus in 1983, following the mass breakout of IRA prisoners from the Maze Prison, the Secretary of State for Northern Ireland refused to accept any constitutional obligation to resign in the absence of proven culpability on his part (which he denied) as distinct from the culpability of civil servants in the Northern Ireland Office: his responsibility for policy had to be distinguished from his responsibility for mere administration. This policy/administration distinction has resurfaced in the light of the "marketising" of the state. It has been asserted that while "the minister is properly accountable for the policies which he settles ... those who have agreed to provide the services are quite properly responsible for their provision" (Waldegrave, 1993).

But the controversy over the management of the Prison Service in 1995, during which the Home Secretary sacked the agency's chief executive, illustrates the strains in the policy/administration distinction.

The Home Secretary, when pressed in the Commons to resign over the mismanagement of the Prison Service, argued that this was the province of the chief executive. Yet the chief executive stated publicly that he had never been able to get to grips with improving management because of constant interference in administration by the Home Office. More importantly, the distinction is only valid if ministers remember that, even if they are no longer under an obligation to resign unless personally at fault for errors of policy, they do retain an obligation to *account* to Parliament, even in respect of matters for which responsibility has been delegated. Sir David Maxwell-Fyfe stressed this: "[The minister alone] remains constitutionally responsible to Parliament for the fact that something has gone wrong, and he alone can tell Parliament what has occurred and render an account of his stewardship." But it is far from clear that the supposedly unimpaired duty to account to Parliament—to provide Parliament with information, to explain and to justify—is being honoured in practice.

---

4. THE COURTS AND THE JUDICIARY

THE JUDICIAL ROLE

The courts are part of the machinery of state as much as Parliament and the government. The key function of the courts is to determine disputes of fact and law. In finding and applying the law, the courts are legally subordinate only to the legislative supremacy of the Queen in Parliament as expressed in statutes. Thus in *Bowles v. Bank of England* (1913) the court refused to accept that a resolution of a committee of the House of Commons assenting to income tax at a certain rate authorised the Crown to levy that tax. That would be possible only when the tax was properly imposed by Act of Parliament.

The discharge of judicial functions is not confined to professional judges sitting in the civil and criminal courts. Schedule 5 to the Judicial Pensions and Retirement Act 1993 refers not only to Lords of Appeal in Ordinary, judges of the Court of Session, sheriffs principal and sheriffs, but also to a great many members of administrative tribunals and to senior public investigative officers, *e.g.* the Parliamentary Commissioner for Administration. Similarly, lay justices of the peace exercise judicial powers in relation to summary criminal justice in the district courts.

JUDICIAL APPOINTMENTS, TENURE AND DISMISSAL

Appointments

Judicial appointments in the United Kingdom are a matter for the executive. There is no independent advisory or appointing body. Lords of Appeal in

Ordinary are appointed by the Queen on the advice of the Prime Minister. Judges of the Court of Session are appointed by the Crown on the advice of the Secretary of State for Scotland, who by convention forwards the nominations submitted to him by the Lord Advocate. Sheriffs principal and sheriffs are also appointed on the advice of the Secretary of State for Scotland. The Secretary of State himself appoints justices of the peace in the name and on behalf of the Queen: District Courts (Scotland) Act 1975, s. 9.

There are, however, certain statutory conditions of eligibility for appointment to judicial office. To be appointed a sheriff principal or sheriff, one must have been legally qualified as a solicitor or advocate for at least 10 years: Sheriff Courts (Scotland) Act 1971, s. 5. Under Article 19 of the Treaty of Union 1707, appointments to the Court of Session bench are governed by a requirement of at least five years' standing as a member of the Faculty of Advocates. This rule was widened by the Law Reform (Miscellaneous Provisions) (Scotland) Act 1990, s. 35(1), which extends eligibility to sheriffs principal or sheriffs who have held office as such for a continuous period of at least five years; and also to solicitors who have enjoyed rights of audience in both the Court of Session and the High Court of Justiciary for at least five years.

Various conventions and practices supplement these rules on judicial appointments. It has been said (Styles, 1988) that there have traditionally been two main paths to the Court of Session bench: the professional route (election as Dean of the Faculty of Advocates) and the political route (service as Lord Advocate or Solicitor-General). If most Court of Session judges arrive *via* the professional route, there is still a significant proportion having a political background. Critics of the existing system of appointments argue that there is nothing formally to prevent political patronage, and that in order to protect the independence of the judiciary an independent body should be established to insulate the appointments process from political influence and control.

Tenure and pay

The historic tenure on which judges in Scotland hold office is *ad vitam aut culpam*—for life or until blame. This was confirmed by Article 13 of the Claim of Right 1689. Security of tenure was and is regarded as a necessary support for judicial independence, and the principle of lifetime tenure was so firmly entrenched that it was held by the Court of Session to attach to any judicial office as a matter of common law right: *Mackay and Esslemont v. Lord Advocate* (1937).

It is of course open to Parliament to override the presumption of the common law. Thus section 26 of the Judicial Pensions and Retirement Act 1993 now prescribes a retirement age of 70 for judges of the Court of Session, sheriffs principal and sheriffs, subject to possible extension to the age of 75 under Schedule 6. Statutes creating new judicial offices are also apt to define tenure in a manner more limited than *ad vitam aut culpam*.

As security of tenure is an important support for judicial independence, so too are judicial salaries. For the same reason that tenure is protected, the

Act of Settlement 1700 provided that judicial salaries should be "ascertained and established"—fixed by statute and not left open to executive discretion. The current position is governed by the Administration of Justice Act 1973, s. 9. This provides that Court of Session judges shall be paid such salaries as may be determined, with the consent of the minister for the civil service, by the Secretary of State. Section 9(2) provides further that any salary payable under this section may be increased but not reduced by further determinations under the section. Judicial salaries are charged on the Consolidated Fund, so that Parliamentary authority for payment is permanent and does not need to be reviewed and renewed year by year.

Dismissal

Section 12 of the Sheriff Courts (Scotland) Act 1971 provides that the Secretary of State may make an order removing a sheriff principal or sheriff from office if, after an inquiry by the Lord President and Lord Justice-Clerk, he or she is found to be unfit for office by reason of inability, neglect of duty or misbehaviour. The order of the Secretary of State is laid before Parliament and is subject to annulment pursuant to a resolution of either the House of Commons or the House of Lords. The procedure has been used twice, in 1977 and again in 1992.

No procedure is prescribed, however, for the dismissal of a Court of Session judge. Article 3 of the Act of Settlement (see now the Supreme Court Act 1981, s. 11) provides that any judge of the Supreme Court of England and Wales except the Lord Chancellor holds office during good behaviour, subject to a power of removal by the Queen on an address presented to her by both Houses of Parliament. The position of the Law Lords is the same: Appellate Jurisdiction Act 1876, s. 6. The procedure has only been used once, in 1830. No Court of Session judge has been dismissed from office since 1688, although one resigned in 1990 following allegations in the press about his private life. In *McCreadie v. Thomson* (1907), the Lord Justice-Clerk appeared to envisage that the English procedure would be adopted in Scotland if necessary. The procedure raises the question, however, of what counts as "good behaviour" and what disqualifies. (It may also be noted that the Scotland Bill, cl. 89, makes provision for the removal from office of a judge of the Court of Session following the establishment of the Scottish Parliament).

JUDICIAL INDEPENDENCE

We have seen that the rules relating to judicial appointments, tenure and dismissal may impinge upon judicial independence. That independence might well be threatened by politically motivated appointments, by removal of security of tenure and manipulation of judicial pay, and by powers of dismissal too frequently exercised. This point denotes the fundamental meaning of judicial independence: freedom from constraint by other institutions of the state. Yet judicial independence has a narrower meaning: a judge's independence of mind in relation to the facts of and parties to a case before him. Some have also argued that the concept has a wider meaning of political neutrality and remoteness from controversy; but it is arguable that this wider meaning is misconceived.

Absence of bias

In the narrowest sense, judicial independence must mean that a judge is impartial. The importance of impartiality has been recognised for a long time: the Declinature Acts of 1594 and 1681 provided that a judge should decline jurisdiction where he was related to one of the parties to a case or where he had some financial interest in its outcome. The common law too enshrines a rule against bias (*nemo judex in causa sua*), because, as Lord Hewart C.J. put it in *R. v. Sussex Justices, ex parte McCarthy* (1924): "It is not merely of some importance, but of fundamental importance that justice should not only be done but should manifestly and undoubtedly be seen to be done."

The rule against bias guards against more than the actual fact of bias. It applies also where bias, on whatever grounds (*e.g.* personal predisposition: *Bradford v. McLeod* (1985); family connections: *Metropolitan Property Co. v. Lannon* (1969); financial interests: *Dimes v. Proprietors of the Grand Junction Canal* (1852)), could reasonably be suspected. In other words, where a judge's decision is challenged on grounds of bias, the test is objective. As the House of Lords held in *R. v. Gough* (1993), the question is not whether the judge was in fact biased, but whether reasonable people would think, in the circumstances, that there was a *real danger* of bias on his part.

Direct political activities

Court of Session judges, sheriffs principal and sheriffs are disqualified from membership of the House of Commons: House of Commons Disqualification Act 1975, s. 1 (although a previous political career, whether as an M.P. or Law Officer, is no bar to appointment to judicial office). Obvious conflicts of constitutional roles would arise if judges were able to be M.P.s. Further, by convention, judges should not become involved in party politics. Thus in 1968, a Court of Session judge, Lord Avonside, was forced to resign from a committee set up by the Leader of the Opposition, Mr Heath, to formulate Conservative policy on the constitutional position of Scotland. In 1977, Sheriff Peter Thomson was dismissed after he was found to have used his judicial office as a platform for the promotion of his political beliefs.

The position differs in the House of Lords. Senior judges such as Lords of Appeal in Ordinary, whose jobs carry with them a life peerage, may sit in the House of Lords and contribute to debates on its legislative business. They sit on the cross-benches rather than as adherents of any political party. The former Lord Justice-Clerk, Lord Wheatley, suggested in 1976 that the proper scope of judicial contribution to legislative debate was limited:

"When the subject enters the political arena and becomes politically controversial, we assume an elective silence on the political issues and confine ourselves, if we intervene at all, to constitutional or legal questions or views on practical matters affecting the law and its administration where our view might naturally be expected and sought."

It is no longer clear that judges see themselves as bound to maintain an "elective silence" in the way that Lord Wheatley suggested. In recent years especially, there have been several instances of retired and serving judges openly criticising government policy in debates on legislation.

Indirect political activities

A number of judicial activities may have indirect political impact. A prominent example is the appointment of judges to conduct public inquiries or to chair commissions, *e.g.* the "Arms to Iraq" inquiry under Scott L.J., and the appointment of Lord Nolan to chair the Committee of Inquiry into Standards in Public Life. The subject-matter of such inquiries is invariably controversial. Appointing a judge to conduct them does not remove the political "sting": where a problem is inherently political, there are no neutral solutions. Thus whatever a judge finds or recommends will inevitably be viewed as politically partial.

Since extra-judicial work on behalf of the government risks undermining the appearance of political impartiality, judges in the United States and Australia generally refuse to serve on government-sponsored inquiries. This emphasises the earlier point that the key to judicial independence is independence from the executive. So far as judicial work of this sort may give the impression of executive influence over the judiciary, it may be inappropriate for judges to undertake it.

Otherwise, judges may contribute to political controversy by expressing their views in the media. In the past, the extent to which judges were able to air their opinions was measured by reference to the so-called "Kilmuir Rules", derived from a letter sent in 1957 by Lord Kilmuir L.C. to the Director-General of the BBC:

"the overriding consideration ... is the importance of keeping the judiciary insulated from the controversies of the day. ... As a general rule it is undesirable for members of the judiciary to broadcast on the wireless or to appear on television. We consider that if judges are approached by the broadcasting authorities with a request to take part in a broadcast on some special occasion, the judge concerned ought to consult the Lord Chancellor."

In time, both the letter and the spirit of the Kilmuir Rules came to look outdated as judges (including Lord Kilmuir) published memoirs, delivered public lectures, wrote for the newspapers and by other means made known their views. In 1987, Lord Mackay L.C. stated that for the future judges would not be required to consult the Lord Chancellor before making public statements. Since then, several judges have asserted claims to a greater degree of autonomous legitimacy than was thought to exist in the past. Recent extra-judicial writings and speeches indicate the emergence, or articulation, of a particular ethic among the ranks of the senior judiciary, which may indeed be reflected in a number of important recent decisions, *e.g. R. v. Home Secretary, ex parte Fire Brigades Union* (1995). It seems that judges do not regard themselves as bound to remain aloof from controversy; on the contrary, they may regard themselves as *entitled*, as judges, to engage in controversial issues.

JUDICIAL INDEPENDENCE IN PERSPECTIVE

Perhaps the main reason why judicial independence is a matter of such importance is that the discharge of judicial functions impinges not only upon disputes between citizens but also upon disputes between citizen and state. To a great extent, it is judges to whom individuals must look for protection of their rights and liberties against intrusion by the state. If they are to fulfil this role, in particular, their independence of mind and freedom from constraint must be assured.

We have seen that a number of positive steps are taken to achieve this end. Tenure and pay are protected and procedures for dismissal of judges are complex—although some would argue that the appointments process does little to assuage fears of executive interference. Bias is impermissible. But partiality in a wider sense is a different matter. It is unrealistic to expect judges to exist in a vacuum of political neutrality, and it is clear that they do not. Professor Griffith draws on cases on, for example, race and sex discrimination, trade union law and police powers to argue that what may be presented as judicial "neutrality" is not in fact neutral at all. On the contrary, Griffith contends that judges—overwhelmingly white, male, middle-aged, middle-class and privately educated—have an inbuilt ideological persuasion tending to coincide, largely, with Conservative politics. Yet it appears that the chief characteristics of the judicial ethic which has been voiced more prominently in recent years are a suspicion of executive power and a commitment to the protection of individual liberties.

Generalising about judicial politics is probably a pointless exercise. What is indisputable is that the judiciary are not without "political" standpoints to which they sometimes give expression. Does this absence of neutrality, and willingness to engage with controversial questions rather than stand remote from them, undermine judicial independence? It is suggested that it does not:

"Public law in general ... exists in a political environment; and the courts in making and applying public law rules perform a variety of political functions. ... It could be argued that ... the ... independence of the judiciary enables the courts to protect certain interests and principles which are of long-term and abiding importance ... from undue encroachment for short-term political reasons" (Cane, 1992).

In so doing, the courts may come into conflict with the executive, but this by itself is not injurious to judicial independence. Quite the reverse: it would tend to emphasise the healthy state of judicial independence, in itself a prerequisite for the rule of law and the checking and balancing of state power.

5. SCOTLAND IN THE UNITED KINGDOM

THE UNITED KINGDOM AS A UNITARY STATE

Despite its historical inheritance, the United Kingdom has a *unitary* constitution, characterised by a single sovereign legislature and a central government. This model of constitutional organisation may be contrasted with the *federal* constitutions of, for example, Germany, Canada and the United States (and, for that matter, the European Union: it may already be true to say that the unitary constitution of the United Kingdom has been absorbed within a European federation). Federal systems are characterised by the entrenched allocation of powers to the central or federal government on the one hand and to regional governments (of *Länder*, provinces or states) on the other. Within their limits, the central and regional governments are independent of one another, in contrast to the hierarchical relationship between central and local government in the United Kingdom. The distribution of powers in a federation, which is invariably contained in a written constitution, is monitored by a supreme court, which ensures that the regional units do not trespass on federal powers and *vice versa*.

Short of federalism, systems of devolved or decentralised government are not uncommon even within unitary states. The arguments for decentralisation are both practical and principled. National, ethnic or linguistic distinctions within a state may underpin decentralised forms of government, as, for example, in Spain. Central authorities may choose to concede some measure of regional autonomy not only to recognise such distinctions but also in order to prevent them from founding claims to independence and secession. In principle, the concept of *subsidiarity* holds that decisions ought to be taken at a level as close as possible to the citizens affected by them. The concept is recognised in the constitutional law of a number of states (*e.g.* Article 72(2) of the German Basic Law). It has also been recognised as a fundamental principle of E.C. law by the European Court of Justice, and is now enshrined in Article 3b(2) of the E.C. Treaty. But subsidiarity is more than an expression of desire for greater "grass roots" democracy. It also acknowledges the fact that many governmental activities are more efficiently and effectively undertaken at a regional or local level than at the centre.

The United Kingdom itself departs in various ways from the strict model of unitary statehood, in a way which goes beyond the well-established structure of local authorities. So far as Scotland is concerned, special provision is made within Parliament for its position. The Secretary of State for Scotland and the Scottish Office represent a substantial degree of administrative devolution. The Scottish and English (and Northern Irish) legal systems remain distinct. And, in recent months, the first steps have been taken towards the establishment of a devolved Scottish Parliament, which may in time move the United Kingdom still further away from the model of unitary statehood in the direction of quasi-federalism, if not independence, for its constituent countries.

SCOTLAND IN PARLIAMENT

Certain special arrangements are made to deal with Scottish legislation at Westminster. The need for special arrangements, a consequence of the distinct Scottish legal system, may sometimes—too often, in the view of some—be accommodated simply by the inclusion of Scottish clauses in legislation primarily applicable in England and Wales. However, there are a number of Scottish institutions within Parliament whose roles have been amplified in recent years in response to growing demands for devolution. Now that those demands have borne fruit, however, it may be that the need for special arrangements at Westminster will diminish.

A Standing Committee for Scottish Bills, consisting of all Scottish M.P.s plus 15 others, was established in 1894 and 1895 to accommodate debate on Scottish affairs, which was being squeezed out by increasing pressure on parliamentary time. The Committee was revived in 1907 as part of a wider review of standing committees in the Commons, and for many years thereafter it undertook the committee stages of Scottish bills after second reading. Discussion of the principles of Scottish bills prior to second reading, and of the Scottish estimates, was added to the Committee's remit in 1948. From 1958, the Scottish Standing Committee acquired a dual identity: as the new Scottish Standing Committee, having a membership of at least 45 Scottish M.P.s, it carried out the committee stage work on Scottish bills; and as the Scottish Grand Committee, retaining the old membership of all Scottish M.P.s plus additional members to maintain party balance, it undertook the other functions of considering bills in principle, estimates, and (which was new) "other matters of particular interest to Scotland". This system continued in existence until 1981.

In 1981, the additional members were removed from the Grand Committee, which was also given authority to sit in Edinburgh. The new system of departmental select committees, including a Select Committee on Scottish Affairs, was also adopted at this time. As Conservative representation in Scotland dwindled throughout the 1980s and 1990s, the functions of the Scottish institutions were enhanced in an effort to quell devolutionary sentiment. Thus changes to the standing orders of the House of Commons in 1995 constituted the Grand Committee as consisting of all Scottish M.P.s and defined its functions to include: questions to Scottish Office ministers and Scottish Law Officers (which supplement monthly Scottish Questions in the Commons and the questioning of ministers by the Select Committee on Scottish Affairs); "short debates" on Scottish matters; consideration of the principles of Scottish legislation; debates on negative or affirmative resolutions on statutory instruments; and adjournment debates. The new standing orders also made provision for the Grand Committee to sit in Scottish towns and cities other than Edinburgh.

THE SCOTTISH OFFICE AND SECRETARY OF STATE FOR SCOTLAND

Central government in the United Kingdom tends to operate on a functional rather than territorial basis. After the Union of 1707, political institutions special to Scotland were largely discouraged. There was, initially, a Scottish Secretary in the new government of Great Britain in London, but the office was abolished in 1746. Thereafter, general responsibility for the government of Scotland was assumed by the Lord Advocate, who was also (and remains) the chief Law Officer of the Crown in Scotland. This state of affairs came to be regarded as inadequate. The continuing distinctiveness of Scots law, coupled with the emergence of Scottish administrative bodies during the nineteenth century, highlighted the absence of a Scottish Cabinet minister able to promote and defend Scottish interests in a British context and generated demands for change.

In response to these demands, the Scottish Office was established in 1885 with a Secretary for Scotland as its ministerial head. Although the Secretary was a Cabinet member from 1892, he was only dignified with the title of Secretary of State for Scotland in 1926, and not until 1937 did the office attract a salary commensurate with those of other Secretaries of State; 1937 brought other changes besides. The *Report of the Gilmour Committee on Scottish Administration* recommended the consolidation within the Scottish Office of all administrative bodies for which the Secretary of State was responsible to Parliament, and the relocation of the Scottish Office itself from Whitehall to Edinburgh. These recommendations were put into effect by the Reorganisation of Offices (Scotland) Act 1939.

Since 1939, the responsibilities of the Secretary of State have increased considerably and now correspond to Scottish affairs which, in functional "United Kingdom" terms, are spread over some nine Whitehall departments. Within the Scottish Office itself there are five functional departments having the following responsibilities:

- Agriculture, Environment and Fisheries Department
- Development Department (housing; local government; town and country planning; transport and roads)
- Education and Industry Department (schools; higher education; training; trade and investment)
- Health Department (hospitals and community health services)
- Home Department (criminal justice, police and prisons).

Executive agencies and non-departmental public bodies linked to the Scottish Office include the Scottish Prison Service, the Scottish Fisheries Protection Agency, the Student Awards Agency for Scotland, Historic Scotland, Scottish Enterprise, Scottish Homes and the Crofters Commission.

To an extent, the Secretary of State for Scotland and the Scottish Office must face in two directions at once, in that while they might for the present be likened to "Scotland's Prime Minister" and "Scotland's government", they are also, respectively, a Cabinet minister and a department of central government. While expected to promote Scotland's interests, the Secretary of State is also subject to the conventions of collective responsibility (which may mean presenting to Scotland policies which do not coincide with Scotland's wishes or preferences) and Cabinet confidentiality (which may make it difficult to guage his effectiveness as Scotland's voice in British government). This duality is particularly apparent when the political complexion of the government of the United Kingdom differs from the political persuasion of Scotland itself. This was notably the case following the general elections of 1987 and 1992, and gave rise in some quarters to the complaint that the Conservative government had no mandate to govern Scotland. Given the current constitutional structure of the United Kingdom, in which all four parts of the United Kingdom are taken, for central government purposes, as one, the "no mandate" argument is misconceived. But the tensions which can arise, and which the argument expresses, are clear; and it is interesting to speculate on the level of tension which would have arisen if, following the 1997 election, in which Scotland returned no Conservative M.P.s at all, a Conservative government had nevertheless been elected on a United Kingdom basis. It is considerations such as these which fuelled the ultimately successful devolution campaign in the 1980s and 1990s.

DEVOLUTION

Devolution was defined by the Royal Commission on the Constitution as "the delegation of central government powers without the relinquishment of sovereignty". This can involve merely the delegation of administrative powers, but it can be taken further to include the delegation of legislative authority.

The Royal Commission on the Constitution was set up, under the chairmanship of Lord Kilbrandon, in response to a surge in Nationalist support in Scotland and Wales in the late 1960s. It reported in 1973. A majority of the Commissioners proposed a scheme of legislative and executive devolution to Scotland (and a bare minority—six out of 13—wished to see this extended to Wales). In 1975, the government outlined its proposals in a white paper, *Our Changing Democracy: Devolution to Scotland and Wales*, which was followed by the introduction of a Scotland and Wales Bill in the House of Commons in 1976. The bill provided for directly elected assemblies in Scotland and Wales, the Scottish Assembly to have legislative powers, the Welsh Assembly to have only executive powers exercisable within the framework of Westminster legislation. Opposed on all sides of the House, the bill was withdrawn after the government moved unsuccessfully to guillotine it. Subsequently, two separate bills for Scotland and Wales were introduced; both were passed, in much amended form, in 1978.

The main features of the Scotland Act were as follows. Given a positive vote in a referendum in Scotland, a Scottish Assembly and Scottish Executive would be set up. This would have no effect on the sovereignty of the Westminster Parliament over the whole of the United Kingdom. The proposed division of powers between Westminster and the Scottish Assembly was complex: the Assembly was to have legislative power in relation to specific "devolved matters", the remainder being the province of Westminster; and even within devolved categories certain subjects remained at the centre. The Secretary of State for Scotland would continue as a Cabinet minister within the central government. He would have power to reserve for Westminster's consideration any bill passed by the Scottish Assembly which in his view strayed into non-devolved matters and which was not in the public interest, and Westminster could by resolution block the submission of the bill for the Royal Assent. He would also have power to veto actions of the Scottish Executive affecting non-devolved matters; and to refer Scottish bills to the Judicial Committee of the Privy Council for a decision on whether it was within the competence of the Assembly. Acts of the Scottish Assembly would remain open to legal challenge after enactment, with final appeal to the Privy Council.

The obscurity and potential for conflict in this scheme are clear. Nor did it all end there. During the passage of the Scotland Bill through Parliament, the M.P. for West Lothian, Mr Tam Dalyell, repeatedly raised the so-called "West Lothian Question": since the bill left Scottish representation at Westminster unaffected, would not Scottish M.P.s be able to interfere in legislation affecting only England, while English M.P.s would have no equivalent right in matters devolved to the Scottish Assembly? A rather bizarre attempt to deal with this problem was made by including an amendment in the bill, against the wishes of the government, which provided that if an "English" bill was approved at second reading only with the support of Scottish M.P.s, a second vote must be held 14 days later (the idea being that Scottish M.P.s could be persuaded to abstain in the meantime).

More significant was the amendment which provided that the Scotland Act should not be put into effect unless a "yes" vote representing 40 per cent of those entitled to vote in the referendum on Scottish devolution was attained. This was to prove crucial. The referendum was held on March 1, 1979, and although 52 per cent of those who actually voted were in favour of devolution, they represented only 33 per cent of the Scottish electorate. Thus, and in accordance with the 1978 Act itself, the Conservative government which took office in May 1979 laid before Parliament an Order in Council to repeal the Act.

The result of the 1979 referendum had, perhaps, less to do with opposition to the principle of devolution than dislike of the model of devolution on offer. The 1970s experiment was not the consequence of a rational assessment of the shortcomings in the United Kingdom's constitutional structure, but an expedient, intended primarily to snuff out rising Nationalist support. Also, by 1978, the government had lost its overall majority in the Commons, rendering the scheme vulnerable to "wrecking" amendments. But the cause was not abandoned after 1979, and was in fact buttressed by a decline in Conservative representation in Scotland throughout the 1980s. This fuelled a perception that Scotland was being ruled from afar by a government with "no mandate" (and a tendency to throw fat on the fire, the early introduction of the poll tax in Scotland being the case in point). The Campaign for a Scottish Assembly was set up in 1979, and its work led to the launch of the Claim of Right in 1988 and the convening of the Scottish Constitutional Convention. The SCC brought together the Labour and Liberal Democrat parties (the SNP and the

Conservatives did not, officially, take part) with a wide variety of other bodies including local authorities, the Scottish Green Party, the Scottish Trades Union Congress, Gaelic organisations and representatives of Scottish churches. The work of the SCC directly informed the proposals of the Labour government elected on May 1, 1997, which almost immediately brought forward legislation providing for referenda in Scotland and Wales on whether a Scottish Parliament and Welsh Assembly respectively should be established. The Scottish referendum held on September 11, 1997 posed two questions: whether there should be a Parliament; and whether it should have tax-varying powers. No 40 per cent threshold was imposed, but it would have made no difference: on a turnout of 60 per cent, three-quarters of those who voted were in favour of the first question, and two-thirds were in favour of the second.

The Scotland Bill received its first reading in the House of Commons on December 17, 1997. It includes the following provisions:

- The Parliament will have 129 members. 73 will be elected by the first past the post method from existing parliamentary constituencies, with Orkney and Shetland constituting two constituencies for this purpose. The remaining 56 "regional" members will be elected according to the additional member system, with seven being returned from each of the eight European Parliamentary constitutencies in Scotland (cl. 1 and Sched.1). Individual candidates may stand for return as constituency members or as regional members. For the election of regional members, a registered political party may submit to the regional returning officer a list of no more than 12 candidates. In the election of regional members, electors may vote either for a party which has submitted a regional list or for an individual candidate. The first regional member seat within a region will be allocated to the party or individual candidate with the highest regional figure. For individual candidates, the regional figure is the total number of votes cast for that candidate in the region. For a political party which has submitted a regional list, the regional figure is the total number of votes cast for the party in the region divided by the aggregate of one plus the number of candidates of the party returned as *constituency* members for constituencies included in the region. When a seat is allocated to a party in this way, its regional figure is recalculated by increasing the aggregate by one. The first regional seat having been allocated, the second and subsequent regional seats will be allocated to the party or individual candidate with the next highest regional figure after any recalculations have been carried out until all seven seats are filled (cls. 4–7).
- Elections to the Parliament will be held on the first Thursday in May every four years. However, the Presiding Officer of the Parliament may request the Crown to dissolve the Parliament and require an extraordinary general election to be held if two-thirds of the MSPs resolve that the Parliament should be dissolved, or if the Parliament

fails to nominate one of its members for appointment as First Minister within 28 days of the office falling vacant (cls. 2–3).

- Under clause 14, those disqualified from membership of the Parliament are persons disqualified from membership of the House of Commons under section 1(1)(a)–(e) of the House of Commons Disqualification Act 1975 (judges, civil servants, members of the armed forces, members of police forces and members of foreign legislatures); persons disqualified from membership of the House of Commons otherwise than under the 1975 Act; Lords of Appeal in Ordinary; and persons who hold an office of a description specified in an Order in Council which may be made under this section. However, clause 15 provides that peers and persons who have been ordained or who are ministers of any religious denomination shall not be disqualified from membership of the Parliament. Citizens of the European Union who are resident in the UK are also eligible to stand for election.

- Clause 18 requires the Parliament to elect from among its members a Presiding Officer and two deputies at its first meeting following a general election.

- Clause 27 provides for the Parliament to enact Acts of the Scottish Parliament. It is stated in clause 27(7) that this section does not affect the power of the Parliament of the UK to make laws for Scotland.

- Clause 28 and Schedule 5 deal with the legislative competence of the Parliament. It is provided that an Act of the Scottish Parliament will not be law so far as any provision of the Act is outside the legislative competence of the Parliament, meaning that it would form part of the law of a country or territory other than Scotland; or that its effect would be to modify any provision of the Scotland Act itself; or that it relates to reserved matters; or that it is incompatible with any of the rights protected by the European Convention on Human Rights or with EC law; or that it would remove the Lord Advocate from his position as head of the system of criminal prosecution and investigation of deaths in Scotland.

- The extensive list of "reserved matters", which remain within the competence of the UK Parliament only, is contained in Schedule 5. It includes, *inter alia*: matters concerning the UK constitution; international relations, including relations with the EU; the civil service; defence; fiscal, economic and monetary policy; the currency; financial services and financial markets; the law on misuse of drugs; data protection law; electoral law; immigration and nationality; national security; emergency powers; trade and industry policy, including company law, insolvency law, competition law, intellectual property law, import and export control and consumer protection; the post office and postal services; energy; rail, marine and air transport; social security; child support; pensions law; the regulation of certain professions; employment law; abortion, embryology, surrogacy and genetics; broadcasting; and further miscellaneous matters including judicial salaries and equal opportunities.

- It is further provided that a provision of an Act of the Scottish Parliament is not to be regarded as incompetent because falling within the sphere of reserved matters merely because it makes modifications of Scots private law or Scots criminal law as it applies to reserved matters if the provision does so in such a way that the law in question applies consistently to devolved and reserved matters (cl. 28(4)). Equally, such a provision will not be incompetent merely because it modifies any enactment as it applies to reserved matters which are *incidental to or consequential on* provision made for purposes relating to devolved matters (cl. 28(5)). Clause 28(9) provides further that any provision of an Act of the Scottish Parliament is *to be read, so far as possible,* so as to be within the legislative competence of the Parliament and is to have effect accordingly. Bear in mind also that an Act of the Scottish Parliament may modify an Act of the UK Parliament, passed or to be passed, if such modification is otherwise within its competence (cl. 28(8)).

- The avoidance of disputes as to competence is dealt with as follows. Clause 30 provides that on or before the introduction of a bill in the Parliament, the member of the Scottish Executive in charge of the bill shall make a statement, in writing, that he regards the bill as falling within the legislative competence of the Parliament. Under Clause 31, the Presiding Officer may nonetheless block the introduction of the bill if he decides that it would not be within the competence of the Parliament; such a determination by the Presiding Officer may, however, be overridden by the Parliament itself.

- The Presiding Officer shall submit bills for the Royal Assent (cl. 31(3)), but he shall not do so if the Advocate General, the Lord Advocate or the Attorney-General is entitled to make a reference in relation to the bill to the Judicial Committee of the Privy Council under section 32; if such a reference has been made; or if an order may be made in relation to the bill by the Secretary of State under section 33. If the Judicial Committee has determined that a bill or any of its provisions would not be within the legislative competence of the Parliament, the Presiding Officer may not submit the bill for the Royal Assent in its unamended form.

- The Advocate General, Lord Advocate or Attorney-General may, under clause 32, refer the question of whether a bill or any of its provisions would be within the competence of the Parliament to the Judicial Committee at any time during the period of four weeks beginning with any subsequent approval by the Parliament of the bill in amended form.

- The Secretary of State may, under clause 33, make an order prohibiting the Presiding Officer from submitting the bill for the Royal Assent if he has reasonable grounds to believe that it would be incompatible with any international obligations, or if he has reasonable grounds to believe that it would have an adverse effect on the operation of an enactment as it applies to reserved matters (even though it is within the competence of the Parliament in terms of clause 28(4) and (5)). Such an order may be made within the same periods as a reference to the Judicial Committee under clause 32.

- The Scottish Executive shall consist of the First Minister, ministers appointed by the First Minister with the approval of the Crown, the Lord Advocate and the Solicitor General for Scotland (cl. 41). The First Minister will be appointed by the Crown on the recommendation of the Presiding Officer, who shall forward to Her Majesty the name of the member of the Scottish Parliament nominated by the Parliament itself. The First Minister and any of the Scottish Ministers may resign at any time, and must do so if the Parliament resolves that the Scottish Executive has lost the confidence of the Parliament.

- Statutory functions may be conferred on the Scottish Ministers by name (cl. 48). Functions of Her Majesty's prerogative and other executive functions exercisable on behalf of Her Majesty by a minister of the Crown and functions conferred on a minister of the Crown by any "pre-commencement enactment" shall, so far as they are exercisable in or as regards Scotland, be exercisable by the Scottish Ministers instead of by a minister of the Crown (with the exception of functions of the Lord Advocate or functions relating to reserved matters) (cl. 49). In accordance with clause 49, functions in relation to observing and implementing obligations under EC law are transferred to the Scottish Ministers; but clause 53 provides that any function of a minister of the Crown in relation to any matter shall continue to be exercisable by him as regards Scotland for the purposes of section 2(2) of the European Communities Act 1972.

- The Parliament will be financed primarily by a Scottish Consolidated Fund, into which the Secretary of State shall from time to time make payments out of moneys provided by the UK Parliament of such amounts as he may determine (cl. 61).

- The power of the Parliament to increase or reduce the basic rate of income tax for Scottish taxpayers, by up to 3 per cent is contained in clause 69. A tax-varying resolution of the Parliament shall relate to no more than a single year of assessment (cl. 70). Only a member of the Scottish Executive may move a motion for a tax-varying resolution. A "Scottish taxpayer" is defined in clause 71 as a person who, in relation to any year of assessment, is an individual who is resident in the UK for income tax purposes in that year, Scotland being the part of the UK with which he has had the "closest connection" during that year.

- Clause 81 provides for the review of Scottish representation at Westminster by the Boundary Commission for Scotland.

- Under Clause 89, it shall continue to be for the Prime Minister to recommend to Her Majesty the appointment of a person as Lord President of the Court of Session or as Lord Justice-Clerk, but he shall not recommend any person who has not been nominated by the First Minister. The First Minister shall recommend to Her Majesty the appointment of a person as any other judge of the Court of Session, a sheriff principal or sheriff. A judge of the Court of Session may be removed from office by Her Majesty on the recommendation of the First Minister, following a resolution voted for by at least two-thirds of the total number of MSPs that the judge in question should be removed from office.

- Clause 91–94 and Schedule 6 deal with judicial scrutiny of devolution issues. A "devolution issue" is defined in paragraph 1(1) of Schedule 6 as a question whether an Act of the Scottish Parliament or any of its provisions is within the legislative competence of the Parliament; whether subordinate legislation which a member of the Scottish Executive has purported to make or proposes to make is or would be within the competence of the Parliament; whether a matter in relation to which a member of the Scottish Executive has purported to exercise or proposed to exercise a function is a reserved matter; whether a purported or proposed exercise of a function by a member of the Scottish Executive is or would be incompatible with any of the Convention rights or with EC law; whether a failure to act by a member of the Scottish Executive is incompatible with any of the Convention rights or with EC law; or whether a matter in relation to which a minister of the Crown has purported to exercise or propose to exercise a function is a devolved matter. A devolution issue shall not be taken to arise in any proceedings if the court or tribunal before which the issue is alleged to arise regards the allegation as frivolous or vexatious.

- In Scotland, proceedings for the determination of a devolution issue may be instituted by the Advocate General or the Lord Advocate (and the Lord Advocate may defend any proceedings instituted by the Advocate General), or by any person. In the latter case, the court or tribunal concerned must intimate to the Advocate General and the Lord Advocate that a devolution issue has been raised in proceedings before it; either or both may be joined as a party to the proceedings so far as they relate to the devolution issue. A court other than the House of Lords or any court consisting of three or more judges of the Court of Session may refer any devolution issue which arises in proceedings (other than criminal proceedings) before it to the Inner House of the Court of Session. A tribunal from which there is no appeal must make such a reference to the Inner House where a devolution issue arises in proceedings before it; any other tribunal may do so. Where a devolution issue arises in criminal proceedings before any court other than a court consisting of two or more judges of the High Court of Justiciary, that court may refer the issue to the High Court of Justiciary. Any court consisting of three or more judges of the Court of Session (or two or more judges of the High Court in criminal proceedings) may refer any devolution issue which arises in proceedings before it (otherwise than on a reference from an inferior court) to the Judicial Committee of the Privy Council; and an appeal against the decision of such a court on a reference from an inferior court shall likewise lie to the Judicial Committee. Separate provision is made for the determination of devolution issues arising in England and Wales and in Northern Ireland.

- Paragraph 32 of Schedule 6 provides that where a devolution issue arises in judicial proceedings in the House of Lords, it shall be referred to the Judicial Committee of the Privy Council unless the House considers it more appropriate, having regard to all the circumstances, that it should determine the issue itself.

- Paragraphs 33–35 of Schedule 6 provide for direct references of devolution issues to the Judicial Committee by the Lord Advocate, the Advocate General, the Attorney-General or the Attorney-General for Northern Ireland.

- Clause 93 provides that where any court or tribunal decides that an Act of the Scottish Parliament or any of its provisions is not within the legislative competence of the Parliament, or that a member of the Scottish Executive does not have the power to make, confirm or approve a provision of subordinate legislation that he has purported to make, confirm or approve, it may make an order removing or limiting any retrospective effect of the decision, or suspending the effect of the decision for any period and on any conditions to allow the defect to be corrected.

The constitutional implications of the establishment of a Scottish Parliament can only be guessed at, as much will depend on the way in which the basic devolution settlement contained in the bill is worked out in practice. Particularly important, perhaps, will be the approach taken by the Privy Council in deciding devolution disputes. A narrow, legalistic approach to the *vires* of Scottish bills or Acts of the Scottish Parliament could undermine the Parliament before it has had time to acquire settled legitimacy and popular support. But there are reasons to suspect that the Privy Council will adopt a more generous and purposive approach than this. The fact that the Scotland Bill proposes to reserve powers to Westminster instead of transferring limited powers to the Scottish Parliament is indicative of a presumption in favour of the validity of Scottish legislation, rebuttable only if the Parliament clearly strays into reserved areas. Such a presumption is reinforced by the principle of subsidiarity, which would provide powerful theoretical justification for an expansive attitude on the Privy Council's part to the competence of the Scottish Parliament. If such an approach *is* adopted, and if as time passes a strong convention develops to restrain Westminster from overriding the Scottish Parliament, the devolution settlement may well come to resemble something closer to federalism than devolution strictly so-called. In that event, the assertion in the Scotland

Bill that the sovereignty of the Westminster Parliament will be unimpaired by the establishment of a Scottish Parliament may well begin to sound somewhat thin.

---

6. PARLIAMENTARY SUPREMACY

THE NATURE OF THE DOCTRINE

Parliamentary supremacy may (still) be regarded as the fundamental principle of the United Kingdom constitution. Historically, the status of Acts of Parliament was questionable: in *Dr Bonham's Case* (1610), Coke C.J. held that "when an Act of Parliament is against common right and reason, or repugnant, or impossible to be performed, the common law will control it, and adjudge such act to be void." However, parliamentary supremacy was implicit in the constitutional settlement following the Glorious Revolution of 1688. From then on, Parliament was the pre-eminent law maker in the state. Its enactments took precedence over and could change the common law and the prerogative.

In 1885, Dicey referred to parliamentary supremacy as "the very keystone of the law of the constitution" and described it in these terms: "Parliament ... has ... the right to make or unmake any law whatever; and ... no person or body is recognised ... as having a right to override or set aside the legislation of Parliament." The principle therefore has a positive and a negative aspect: on the one hand, Parliament has absolute legislative competence; on the other, no court or other body may question the validity of its legislation.

It is implicit in this that it is the *current* Parliament which is supreme. It therefore follows that any conflict between an Act of the current Parliament and an Act of one of its predecessors must be resolved in favour of the former: the later statute *impliedly repeals* the earlier. In Dicey's theory, the only limitation on Parliament's absolute legislative authority is its inability to bind its successors: "The logical reason why Parliament has failed in its endeavours to enact unchangeable enactments is that a sovereign power cannot, while retaining its sovereign character, restrict its own powers by a parliamentary enactment."

In *Ellen Street Estates v. Minister of Health* (1934), Maugham L.J. agreed:

"The legislature cannot ... bind itself as to the form of subsequent legislation, and it is impossible for Parliament to enact that in a subsequent statute dealing with the same subject-matter there can be no implied repeal. If in a subsequent Act Parliament chooses to make it plain that the earlier statute is being to some extent repealed, effect must be given to that intention just because it is the will of Parliament."

There is evidence supportive of both the positive and negative aspects of Dicey's theory. It has been said that "one does not establish that Parliament can do anything merely by pointing to a number of things that it has done, however impressive" (Munro, 1987), but the fact that, so far, Parliament has not done certain things does not necessarily disprove Dicey's theory either. So at least some support for the assertion of unlimited legislative competence may be drawn from the many statutes whereby Parliament has made important constitutional changes (*e.g.* the Reform Act 1832; the Irish Free State (Constitution) Act 1922); enacted retrospective legislation (*e.g.* the War Damage Act 1965); or legislated extra-territorially (*e.g.* the War Crimes Act 1991).

Authority for the negative aspect is found in cases concerning the "enrolled bill rule". In *Edinburgh and Dalkeith Ry v. Wauchope* (1842) Lord Campell stated this rule as follows:

"All that a Court of Justice can do is look to the Parliamentary Roll; if from that it should appear that a Bill has passed both Houses and received the Royal Assent, no Court of Justice can inquire into the mode in which it was introduced into Parliament, nor into what was done previous to its introduction, or what passed in Parliament during its progress ... through Parliament."

More recently, in *Pickin v. British Railways Board* (1974), Mr Pickin asked the court to hold a private Act void on the grounds that the Board had procured its enactment by misleading Parliament and that the standing orders of both Houses had not been properly followed. The House of Lords held that the courts had no power to disregard an Act of Parliament whether public or private, or to inquire into parliamentary procedures. As Willes J. held in *Lee v. Bude and Torrington Junction Ry* (1871): "If an Act of Parliament has been obtained improperly, it is for the legislature to correct it by repealing it; but so long as it exists as law, the courts are bound to obey it."

The courts have also rejected substantive (as distinct from procedural) arguments to the effect that Parliament lacked authority to legislate. In *Cheney v. Conn* (1968) it was argued that assessments of tax under a Finance Act were made partly for a purpose which was unlawful as being contrary to international law. Ungoed-Thomas J. held: "What the statute itself enacts cannot be unlawful, because [it] is the highest form of law that is known to this country ... and it is not for the court to say that a parliamentary enactment ... is illegal."

Two basic points should be stressed:

- The doctrine of parliamentary supremacy is a purely legal construct. It denotes the absence of *legal* limitations on Parliament's legislative competence; it does *not* argue that Parliament is unrestrained by political or practical considerations.
- The essence of the doctrine lies in its account of the relationship between Parliament and the courts, and the effect to be given by the courts to

Acts of Parliament. The doctrine is a product of the common law: one might therefore say that its continuing truth "lies in the keeping of the courts" (Wade, 1955).

A number of arguments challenge Dicey's theory. These are, first, that the Acts of Union constitute "fundamental law" which Parliament cannot contradict; secondly, that Parliament *has* restricted its legislative competence, notably in the context of the legislation conferring independence on former colonies; thirdly, that even if Parliament cannot restrict its substantive competence, it could bind itself as to the "manner and form" of subsequent legislation; and fourthly, that the United Kingdom's accession to the European Communities in 1973 has modified parliamentary supremacy. We shall consider these in turn.

THE ACTS OF UNION AS FUNDAMENTAL LAW

It has been argued that the 1707 Treaty of Union, in creating a Parliament for Great Britain, also limited the powers of the new institution. Parliament cannot enjoy unfettered legislative competence because it was "born unfree" (Smith, 1957; Mitchell, 1968). This argument draws on the special nature of the union legislation as fundamental and constituent, and also upon indications in the language of the legislation that parts of it, at least, were intended to be unalterable.

Dicey conceded that the framers of the union legislation may well have sought to give certain provisions more than the ordinary effect of statutes, but: "the history of legislation in respect of these very Acts affords the strongest proof of the futility inherent in every attempt of one sovereign legislature to restrain the action of another equally sovereign legislature."

Here Dicey was referring to the Anglo-Irish as well as the Anglo-Scottish union legislation. The Union with Ireland Act 1800 contained language similar to that of the 1707 Treaty. Quite clearly, it failed to have the desired effect: the union itself was dissolved (partially) by an ordinary statute, the Irish Free State (Constitution) Act 1922. While the Anglo-Scottish union remains intact, it is nonetheless true that nearly all of the provisions of the 1707 Treaty have been repealed or amended.

Some Scottish cases contain dicta sympathetic to the fundamental law argument. In *MacCormick v. Lord Advocate* (1953) Lord President Cooper observed:

"The principle of the unlimited sovereignty of Parliament is a distinctively English principle which has no counterpart in Scottish constitutional law. … I have difficulty in seeing why it should have been supposed that the new Parliament of Great Britain must inherit all the peculiar characteristics of the English Parliament but none of the Scottish Parliament, as if all that happened in 1707 was that Scottish representatives were admitted to the Parliament of England. That is not what was done."

But, having apparently accepted that certain provisions of the Treaty were to be regarded as unalterable, his Lordship then seemed to doubt whether an allegation of breach of that fundamental law would be "determinable as a justiciable issue in the courts of either Scotland or England". Similarly in *Gibson v. Lord Advocate* (1975), Lord Keith reserved his opinion as to the effect of hypothetical Acts of Parliament purporting to abolish the Church of Scotland or the Court of Session, but held that arguments about whether changes to Scots private law were "for the evident utility" of the subjects in Scotland in accordance with Article XVIII of the Treaty of Union, would not be justiciable. More explicitly, Lord Kirkwood stated in *Murray v. Rogers* (1992) that "there is ... no machinery whereby the validity of an Act of Parliament can be brought under review by the courts". Thus, even if there is force in the fundamental law argument in the abstract sense, it is of little use if the courts will not treat such issues as justiciable.

THE "END OF EMPIRE" ARGUMENT

Dicey asserted an absence only of legal limitations on Parliament's legislative competence. Yet the distinction between Parliament being legally unlimited and illimitable on the one hand, but politically constrained on the other may seem rather unreal when set against the dismantling of the British Empire. In this context, does it make sense to speak of one Parliament undoing the work of its predecessors by purporting to reassume legislative authority over former colonies? If it does not make sense, it would seem to follow that earlier Parliaments have bound their successors.

Section 4 of the Statute of Westminster 1931 provided that no future Act of Parliament would extend or be deemed to extend to a Dominion (including Canada, Australia, New Zealand and South Africa) unless it was expressly declared in the Act that the Dominion had requested and consented to its enactment. In enacting section 4, did Parliament deprive itself of the competence to legislate in future for a Dominion, even without the Dominion's request? In *British Coal Corporation v. R.* (1935), Lord Sankey L.C. remarked that:

"It is doubtless true that the power of the Imperial Parliament to pass on its own initiative any legislation it thought fit extending to Canada remains in theory unimpaired: indeed the Imperial Parliament could as a matter of abstract law repeal or disregard section 4 of the Statute. But that is theory and has no relation to realities."

Less equivocally still, Stratford A.C.J. held in the South African case of *Ndlwana v. Hofmeyr* (1937) that "freedom once conferred cannot be revoked". The "end of empire" argument suggests, then, that the conferment of independence on former colonies involved an irrevocable abdication by Parliament of its sovereignty in relation to those countries.

If Parliament were to repeal, for example, the Canada Act 1982, and purported to legislate again for Canada, the Canadian courts would, no doubt, completely ignore such legislation. But the Diceyan concept of parliamentary supremacy addresses the relationship between Parliament and *United Kingdom* courts: would the courts of Scotland, England and Northern Ireland treat such legislation as valid? The authorities suggest that they would.

For example, in 1965, the government of Southern Rhodesia unilaterally declared independence. In the Southern Rhodesia Act 1965, Westminster reasserted its right to legislate for the territory, and in *Madzimbamuto v. Lardner-Burke* (1969), the Privy Council held that emergency regulations made by the rebel regime were void and that the provisions of United Kingdom statutes continued to have full legal force in Rhodesia. Be that as it may, the Rhodesian courts did not accept the decisions of the Privy Council as binding on them following the declaration of independence, and held in *R. v. Ndhlovu* (1968) that the revolutionary constitution of 1965 was the only lawful constitution of Rhodesia. But that does not alter the fact that whatever Acts Parliament might have enacted for Rhodesia, the British courts would have recognised them as valid and obeyed them.

Again, in *Manuel v. Att.-Gen.* (1983), Canadian Indian chiefs contended that the Canada Act 1982, which "patriated" the Canadian constitution, was *ultra vires* and void. Megarry V.-C. held:

"I have grave doubts about the theory of the transfer of sovereignty as affecting the competence of Parliament. ... As a matter of law the courts ... recognise Parliament as being omnipotent in all save the power to destroy its own omnipotence. Under the authority of Parliament the courts of a territory may be released from their legal duty to obey Parliament, but that does not trench on the acceptance by the English courts of all that Parliament does. *Nor must validity in law be confused with practical enforceability* [emphasis added]."

Although there is no direct Scottish authority on this point, there is little reason to believe that the Scottish courts would not hold likewise.

THE NEW VIEW: "MANNER AND FORM" RESTRICTIONS

It has been argued that, while the doctrine of parliamentary supremacy may prevent Parliament from binding itself as to the content of future legislation, it does not prevent "manner and form" fetters (Jennings, 1959; Heuston, 1964). On this view, should Parliament wish to entrench an incorporated European Convention on Human Rights, it could provide in the incorporating Act that none of its provisions shall be repealed or amended without, for example, a two-thirds majority vote in both Houses of Parliament.

The evidence relied on for this "new view" of parliamentary supremacy is derived primarily from Commonwealth cases, notably *Att.-Gen. for New South Wales v. Trethowan* (1932) and *Bribery Commissioner v. Ranasinghe* (1965), both decisions of the Privy Council; and the South African case of *Harris v. Minister of the Interior* (1952).

In *Harris*, the Union Parliament of South Africa passed by simple majority, both Houses sitting separately, the Separate Representation of Voters Act 1951 pursuant to the new *apartheid* policy. Voters thereby deprived of their voting rights argued that the Act was invalid because contrary to section 35 of the South Africa Act 1909 (an Act of the United Kingdom Parliament). Section 35 required certain legislation of the South African Parliament, including the 1951 Act, to be "passed by both Houses of Parliament *sitting together*, and at third reading ... *agreed to by not less than two-thirds of the total number of members of both Houses* [emphasis added]." The South African government argued that the Union Parliament had since 1909 acquired full legislative sovereignty and so was free to disregard purported limitations on its sovereignty contained in section 35. Unanimously, the court rejected this argument and held the 1951 Act *ultra vires* and void. Centlivres C.J. stated that:

"A State can unquestionably be sovereign although it has no legislature which is completely sovereign. ... In the case of the Union, legal sovereignty is or may be divided between Parliament as ordinarily constituted and Parliament as constituted under [section 35]. Such a division of legislative powers is no derogation from the sovereignty of the Union and the mere fact that that division was enacted in a British statute which is still in force in the Union cannot affect the question in issue. ... The South Africa Act ... created the Parliament of the Union. It is that Act ... which prescribes the manner in which the constituent elements of Parliament must function for the purpose of passing legislation. ... [I]t follows that ... courts of law have the power to declare the Act of 1951 invalid on the ground that it was not passed in conformity with the provisions of section 35."

This passage illustrates the crux of the manner and form theory. In identifying expressions of the sovereign will as an Act of Parliament, the courts need a rule, or rules, of recognition (Hart, 1994). Among other things, they need a rule defining what we mean by "Parliament" if they are correctly to identify one of its Acts. In *Harris*, the constituent instrument of the Union Parliament contained such rules for the guidance of the courts in particular instances. Thus where an "Act of Parliament" is enacted by simple majority, both Houses sitting separately, in an area where the governing instrument defines "Parliament" as both Houses sitting together and acting by a two-thirds majority, it is both right and logical for the courts to hold that what purports to be an "Act of Parliament" is *not*, in this instance, an Act of Parliament at all.

And yet this tells us little about the United Kingdom Parliament because, as Lord Pearce put it in *Ranasinghe*: "In the United Kingdom there is no governing instrument which prescribes the law-making powers and the forms which are essential to those powers."

But the new view goes further. If the "United Kingdom Parliament" is bound by no definitions in any constituent instrument, its meaning is nonetheless subject to *common law* rules relied on by the courts in the identification of statutes. As a matter of common law, the courts accept that whatever the Queen in Parliament enacts, both Houses of Parliament sitting separately and acting by simple majority, is law. We know, however, that Parliament can change the common law. It must therefore follow that Parliament can change this common law rule and, in certain circumstances, substitute a different definition of what Parliament is for the purpose of identifying a valid Act of Parliament.

In truth, however, it may not so follow:

"[T]he rule that the courts obey Acts of Parliament ... is above and beyond the reach of statute ... because it is itself the source of authority of statute. This puts it into a class by itself among rules of the common law ... . The rule of judicial obedience is in one sense a rule of common law, but in another sense—which applies to no other rule of common law—it is the ultimate *political* fact upon which the whole system of legislation hangs. Legislation owes its authority to the rule: the rule does not owe its authority to legislation. To say that Parliament can change the rule ... is to put the cart before the horse. ... The rule is unique in being unchangeable by Parliament — it is changed by revolution, not by legislation; it lies in the keeping of the courts and no Act of Parliament can take it from them" (Wade, 1955).

Such a revolution occurred in Rhodesia, when the Rhodesian courts ceased to recognise British statutes as supreme and relocated their rules of recognition—their criteria of legal validity—in the revolutionary constitution of 1965. The same sort of process occurred in the Glorious Revolution of 1688, whereby James VII of Scotland and II of England was deposed, William and Mary were offered the Crown and the Parliaments of both countries asserted their pre-eminence in, respectively, the Claim of Right and the Bill of Rights. By the standards of the time, all of these acts were illegal. Yet in 1688 the pre-existing legal order was comprehensively overturned. By what standard then can it be said that what happened in 1688, and what has happened since, is legal? The answer to this lies in the acquiescence of the courts in the "break in legal continuity" occasioned by new political realities and in their acceptance of a new criterion of legal validity, namely the legal supremacy of Parliament.

Does this mean that, however much Parliament may wish to entrench a Bill of Rights in the future, it is simply unable to do so—or unable to do so without a "revolution"? Professor Wade himself refuted this notion:

"Even without a [break in legal continuity] there might be a shift in judicial loyalty if we take into account the dimension of time. ... [N]ew generations of judges might come to accept that there had been a new constitutional settlement based on common consent and long usage, and that the old doctrine of sovereignty was ancient history ... . The judges would then be adjusting their doctrine to the facts of constitutional life, as they have done throughout history" (Wade, 1989).

The courts have already made such an adjustment in respect of the impact of E.C. law.

THE EFFECT OF EUROPEAN COMMUNITY LAW

The United Kingdom became a member of the European Communities on January 1, 1973. European Community law is derived primarily from the founding treaties which established the European Communities, *e.g.* the 1957 Treaty of Rome; and from the treaties which have since amended the founding treaties, notably the Single European Act 1986; the Treaty on European Union signed at Maastricht in 1992; and the 1997 Treaty of Amsterdam, which takes the process of European integration still further. European Community law also consists of acts of the Community institutions which have legal force: regulations, directives and decisions. Treaties entered into by the Community with third states also become part of E.C. law; and the European Court of Justice (ECJ) has held that rules of E.C. law may also be derived from "general principles of law common to the member states".

On accession to treaties, member states are obliged by Article 5 of the Treaty of Rome to "take all appropriate measures ... to ensure fulfilment of the obligations arising out of this Treaty or resulting from action taken by the institutions of the Community". As a matter of British constitutional law, treaties signed and ratified by the government have no domestic legal impact unless and until incorporated by Act of Parliament. The European Communities Act 1972 was therefore enacted to incorporate E.C. law and to enable the United Kingdom to fulfil the further obligations of membership.

Section 1 defines the Community treaties being incorporated and provides that the government may by Order in Council declare other treaties to be Community treaties for the purposes of the Act. Section 2 then provides for the whole body of E.C. law, including future accretions to that body of law, to be applied in United Kingdom courts. Section 2(4) is especially worthy of note. It provides that "any enactment passed or to be passed ... shall be construed and have effect subject to the foregoing provisions of this section", that is, subject to E.C. law as incorporated in accordance with section 2(1). Section 3 provides that in all legal proceedings in the United Kingdom, any questions as to the meaning or effect of E.C. law shall be determined in accordance with the jurisprudence of the ECJ.

What, then, is the relationship between E.C. law and national law? It must be stressed at the outset that E.C. law is, to put it mildly, a distinctive species of international law. As the ECJ asserted in *Van Gend en Loos* (1963): "The Community constitutes a new legal order of international law *for the benefit of which states have limited their sovereign rights* [emphasis added]."

This pronouncement of the autonomy of E.C. law was shortly followed by a pronouncement of its primacy in *Costa v. ENEL* (1964):

"The transfer by the states from their domestic legal systems to the Community legal system of the rights and obligations arising under the Treaty carries with it a *permanent limitation of their sovereign rights, against which a subsequent unilateral act incompatible with the concept of the Community cannot prevail* [emphasis added]."

The ECJ later held in *Internationale Handelsgesellschaft* (1970) that E.C. law in all its forms prevails even over conflicting provisions of national constitutions. It also prevails whether the conflicting national law was made before or after the relevant provisions of E.C. law, as the ECJ made clear in *Simmenthal* (1978):

"every national court must ... apply Community law in its entirety and protect rights which the latter confers on individuals, and must accordingly set aside any provision of national law which may conflict with it, whether prior or subsequent to the Community rule."

Thus where E.C. law and national law clash, it is the duty of national courts to "disapply" national law to the extent of the conflict. The challenge to traditional notions of parliamentary supremacy—that Parliament has unlimited legislative competence, and that no court is able to question an Act of Parliament—is obvious. The question is whether there is any way of reconciling Diceyan doctrine with the primacy of E.C. law.

Without the European Communities Act 1972, E.C. law would never have become part of the law of the United Kingdom. It was that Act which, by incorporating E.C. law, made it domestically binding and enforceable. However, the very fact that an Act of Parliament was necessary to achieve this would seem to leave E.C. law vulnerable to a future Act of Parliament which contradicted it. The role of national courts as traditionally understood is to give effect to the latest expression of the sovereign will of Parliament. That, one might argue, remains the case even though the 1972 Act itself directs the United Kingdom courts to enforce any measures of E.C. law which have created enforceable individual rights.

For practical purposes, the courts have effected a reconciliation by adopting a special principle of statutory construction in this field. In *Macarthys v. Smith* (1979), a conflict existed between Article 119 of the Treaty of Rome, concerning equal pay, and section 1 of the Equal Pay Act 1970. Lord Denning M.R. held that:

"Under section 2(1) and (4) of the European Communities Act 1972 the principles laid down in the Treaty are 'without further enactment' to be given legal effect in the UK; and have priority over 'any enactment passed or to be passed' by our Parliament. ... In construing our statute, we are entitled to look to the Treaty as an aid to its construction; but not only as an aid but as an overriding force. If ... it should appear that our legislation is deficient or is inconsistent with Community law by some oversight of our draftsmen then it is our bounden duty to give priority to Community law. Such is the result of section 2(1) and (4) of the European Communities Act 1972."

Thus the courts will presume that any inconsistency with E.C. law contained in a British statute was unintended and accidental. The courts are therefore doing no more than fulfilling Parliament's real and genuine intention—to comply with E.C. law—in overriding the domestic provision.

In *Macarthys*, however, the incompatibility was contained in a statute pre-dating the European Communities Act 1972. It could therefore be argued that section 1 of the Equal Pay Act 1970 had been impliedly repealed by the 1972 Act and, as such, by E.C. law. More important is the question of how the courts treat a subsequent statute which conflicts with E.C. law.

The Merchant Shipping Act 1988 laid down nationality requirements for the registration of fishing vessels. These requirements could not be met by a number of vessels owned by English companies whose management and shareholders were primarily Spanish nationals. The vessels were therefore deprived of their right to exploit the fishing quotas assigned to the United Kingdom under the Common Fisheries Policy. The companies sought judicial review of the legality of the legislation, contending that it contravened several provisions of the Treaty of Rome. The ECJ held in *R. v. Transport Secretary, ex parte Factortame (No. 2)* (1991) that the legislation was incompatible with E.C. law. The case was returned to the House of Lords, where Lord Bridge held:

"Some public comments on the decision of the Court of Justice ... have suggested that this was a novel and dangerous invasion by a Community institution of the sovereignty of the UK Parliament. But such comments are based on a misconception. If the supremacy within the European Community of Community law over the national law of member states was not always inherent in the EEC Treaty it was certainly well-established in the jurisprudence of the Court of Justice long before the UK joined the Community. *Thus whatever limitation of its sovereignty Parliament accepted when it enacted the European Communities Act 1972 was entirely voluntary* [emphasis added]. Under the terms of the 1972 Act it has always been clear that it was the duty of a UK court, when delivering final judgment, to override any rule of national law found to be in conflict with any directly enforceable rule of Community law."

The House of Lords has since held that there is no constitutional bar which prevents an individual directly seeking judicial review of primary legislation which is alleged to be in breach of E.C. law before the United Kingdom courts: *R. v. Employment Secretary, ex parte Equal Opportunities Commission* (1995).

Where does this leave us? As a matter of national law, the courts have accepted the supremacy of E.C. law over Acts of Parliament whether enacted prior or subsequent to the relevant Community provisions. In either case, it is presumed that Parliament did not intend to contravene E.C. law. Thus it is not open to Parliament *impliedly* to repeal E.C. law or, for that matter, the European Communities Act 1972 (which raises interesting questions about the status of the 1972 Act—the only British statute, it would seem, which is resistant to implied repeal). The principle of parliamentary supremacy has therefore been modified—at least for the time being—to this extent: we must now say that Parliament has unlimited legislative competence and no court may question or set aside an Act of Parliament *except* where E.C. law applies, in which case E.C. law prevails and the courts have jurisdiction to declare an Act of Parliament to be incompatible with E.C. law.

The as yet unanswered question is what would happen if Parliament chose *expressly* to derogate from E.C. law, by, say, providing in some hypothetical statute that "for the purposes of this Act, the European Communities Act 1972 shall be disregarded". Lord Denning M.R. addressed this issue in *Macarthys*:

"If the time should come when our Parliament deliberately passes an Act with the intention of repudiating the Treaty or any provision of it or intentionally of acting inconsistently with it and says so in express terms then I should have thought that it would be the duty of our courts to follow the statute of our Parliament."

The ECJ, of course, sees the matter differently. An argument from a "Community" angle might therefore assert that United Kingdom courts would be obliged to "disapply" even an Act of Parliament which expressly contradicts E.C. law: if the United Kingdom wishes to depart from its obligations as a member state, it must negotiate for release from the Community and for the restoration of the sovereignty which it is said to have transferred to the Community on accession. This argument would lend credence to Professor Wade's thesis that changes to the principle of parliamentary supremacy "lie in the keeping of the courts" (although in *Factortame*, Lord Bridge was careful to ascribe the constitutional consequences of United Kingdom membership of the Community to Parliament's own choice in 1972; the courts might, understandably, prefer to characterise the whole issue as one which lies in the keeping of Parliament).

The question of the effect of a purported express departure from E.C. law remains to be addressed. It may never be addressed. But it is arguable that, the longer the United Kingdom remains a member of the Community and honours its obligations as a member state, the likelier it is that United Kingdom courts will insist—on grounds of the rule of law, if nothing else—that partial compliance with E.C. law, even if ordained expressly by statute, is not legally possible.

---

7. PRINCIPLES OF CONSTITUTIONAL GOVERNMENT

The term "constitutionalism" denotes a particular conception of the relationship between the state and individual citizens. It is both a descriptive concept and an aspirational one: descriptive in that it is reflected in actual constitutional practice; aspirational in that it also guides and influences constitutional practice. Constitutionalism has a long historical pedigree, for it has been recognised since ancient times that while genuine individual freedom in a community of persons requires rule-making and rule-enforcing institutions, the powers of government may be used not to promote individual freedom but to restrict and oppress it. Theories of constitutionalism therefore seek to reconcile the need for order and government with the preservation of liberty. This reconciliation is achieved, broadly speaking, by using law to empower, guide and restrain both government and citizens. Crucial principles bound up in the notion of constitutionalism are the rule of law and the separation of powers.

THE RULE OF LAW

The basic idea of the rule of law is the subjection of power to legal limits. In Dicey's view, the rule of law was one of the cornerstones of the constitution and had been since the Revolution of 1688 put an end to the claims of the Stuarts to rule by prerogative right and ushered in the modern era of parliamentary supremacy. Judicial affirmation of the rule of law in this sense came in *Entick v. Carrington* (1765). There, the Secretary of State had issued a warrant ordering the King's Messengers to break into Entick's house and seize his books and papers. When sued for damages, it was claimed that the warrant was valid authority for the Messengers' actions, a power of seizure being necessary for the ends of government. Lord Camden C.J. rejected this argument in the following terms:

"every invasion of private property ... is a trespass. No man can set his foot upon my ground without my licence, but he is liable to an action. ... If he admits the fact, *he is bound to show by way of justification that some positive law has empowered or excused him. The justification is submitted to the judges, who are to look into the books, and see if such a justification can be maintained by the text of the statute law, or principles of the common law* [emphasis added]. ... It is said that it is necessary for the ends of government to lodge such a power with a state officer ... but with respect to the argument of state necessity, or to a distinction that has been aimed at between state offences and others, the common law does not understand that kind of reasoning, nor do our books take notice of any such distinctions."

In his exposition of the rule of law, Dicey went beyond this basic principle of legality. There are three facets to Dicey's theory:

- He took the rule of law to mean, first, "the absolute supremacy or predominance of regular law as opposed to the influence of arbitrary power". Arbitrariness, prerogative, even "wide discretionary authority on the part of the government" he regarded as incompatible with the rule of law.

- The rule of law also denoted equality before the law, meaning "the equal subjection of all classes to the ordinary law of the land administered by the ordinary law courts". Where the rule of law was observed, officials and private citizens alike were subject to the same legal rules before the same courts.

- Thirdly, the rule of law meant that "with us the law of the constitution … [is] not the source but the consequence of the rights of individuals, as defined and enforced by the courts." Dicey regarded the British constitution as being the product of the ordinary law, developed by the courts on a case by case basis, as contrasted with a constitutional order superimposed from above in the manner of a written constitution. Individual rights were not conferred by a constitutional document, but were secured by the availability of ordinary legal remedies to those whose rights had been unlawfully infringed.

Many criticisms may be made of Dicey's account. First, few would accept today that discretionary governmental powers are incompatible with the rule of law. In the modern interventionist state—as distinct from the "nightwatchman state" of the nineteenth century—discretionary powers are both prevalent and necessary. Moreover, as discretionary powers have their source in statutes—"regular law"—they have unquestionable legal pedigree themselves. Constitutionalism does not require us to get rid of discretionary power, but to develop appropriate legal and political controls by which to regulate its exercise.

Secondly, Dicey's emphasis on equality before the law stemmed from his aversion to the separation of public and private law in France. He considered that the French system of administrative courts protected officials and disfavoured the citizen. This viewpoint is misconceived. Separate administrative courts may offer protection to the citizen as well as, if not better than, ordinary courts. In any event, the Crown enjoys a number of immunities in the United Kingdom which diminish the force of Dicey's assertion of equality before the law: *e.g. Lord Advocate v. Dumbarton D.C.* (1990), which affirmed the rule that the Crown is not subject to any burden imposed by a statute unless the statute says it is to be bound in express terms or by necessary implication.

As to Dicey's third meaning of the rule of law, it is questionable whether his "judge-made constitution" is adequate to the task of protecting individual freedom from state power. Ordinary common law remedies were of no help in *Malone v. Metropolitan Police Commissioner* (1979). There, with the permission of the Post Office (which was at that time in charge of telecommunications), the police had tapped Mr Malone's telephone. The police had no positive legal authority to do this. However, there was nothing to stop them doing it: as tapping telephones involved no invasion of property rights, and since the common law recognises no right of privacy, Mr Malone was denied a remedy (although in *Malone v. U.K.* (1984) the European Court of Human Rights held that the United Kingdom was in breach of the right of privacy enshrined in Article 8 of the European Convention).

Furthermore, as Acts of Parliament override the common law, it has always been possible for Parliament to restrict or remove fundamental freedoms by statute. Parliamentary supremacy was the other cornerstone of the Diceyan constitution, but if the rule of law means merely that oppressive executive actions be clothed with legality by statute, it amounts to little guarantee of individual liberty in a system where Parliament is supreme and where it is possible for the government to harness that supremacy to its own ends. The extent to which incorporation of the European Convention on Human Rights in 1998 will alter this position remains to be seen.

As a constitutional principle, the rule of law has great resonance and moral authority as a tool of criticism of constitutional practice. It has rightly been described as a principle of "institutional morality" (Jowell, 1993). Not surprisingly, then, there has been much debate about the content of the principle and about how much work it can be made to do. A distinction to be drawn here is that between *formal* and *substantive* conceptions of the rule of law. Formal conceptions focus on matters of procedure rather than matters of substance or the content of laws:

"If the rule of law is the rule of the good law, then to explain its nature is to propound a complete social philosophy. But if so, the term lacks any useful function. We have no need to be converted to the rule of law just in order to discover that to belive in it is to believe that good should triumph" (Raz, 1977).

The formal rule of law therefore embodies politically neutral values, which because of their neutrality may be universally acceptable. Laws should be general, not discriminatory; open, not secret; clear, not obscure in their meaning; stable, not forever changing; and prospective rather than retrospective in application. To ensure conformity with these standards, the independence of the judiciary must be assured, the principles of natural justice must be observed and access to justice must be guaranteed. Compliance with these values enables officials and private citizens alike to plan their conduct in a rational way.

Critics of this approach argue that such formalism is compatible with iniquitous legal systems such as those of the Third Reich or South Africa under apartheid. It has also been said that the formal rule of law is a "legitimating device" which blinds people to real, substantive inequalities in society and so shores up the control of a political elite. Indeed, some theorists have altogether rejected the notion that a distinction can be drawn between the form and substance of law, contending that even the "neutral" values of the formal rule of law are derived from particular moral and political precepts. Substantive conceptions of the rule of law therefore subscribe to the values included in formal conceptions, but:

"they wish to take the doctrine further. Certain substantive rights are said to be based on, or derived from, the rule of law. The concept is used as the foundation for these rights, which are then used to distinguish between 'good' laws, which comply with such rights, and 'bad' laws, which do not" (Craig, 1997).

In defence of the formalists, however, substantive conceptions could be accused of attempting to attach the moral persuasion of the term "rule of law" to their own preferred political theories, thereby rendering the doctrine unhelpfully contingent upon subjective viewpoints. In insisting on the independent and general functions of the rule of law, formalists have made clear that the rule of law is not the only attribute which a "good" constitution should possess. There are other worthy attributes to which to aspire— democracy, justice, equality, a Bill of Rights—but these are not to be confused with, or seen to be required by, the rule of law itself.

THE SEPARATION OF POWERS

The classic statements of the separation of powers doctrine came in the seventeenth and eighteenth centuries. In his *Second Treatise on Civil Government* (1690), Locke said: "It may be too great a temptation to human frailty, apt to grasp at power, for the same persons who have the power of making laws to have also in their hands the power to execute them."
  In *The Spirit of the Laws* (1748), Montesquieu wrote:

"In every government there are three sorts of power ... that of making laws, that of executing public affairs and that of adjudicating on crimes and individual causes. ... When the legislative and executive powers are united in the same person or in the same body of magistrates, there can be no liberty. ... Again, there is no liberty if the power of judging is not separated from the legislative and executive. ... There would be an end to everything if the same man or the same body ... were to exercise those three powers."

Implicit in this is the crucial evil which the separation of powers doctrine seeks to avoid: the monopolisation of the powers of the state in too few hands, with all that that implies in terms of loss of liberty. The powers of the state are therefore divided into three categories—legislative, executive and judicial powers—and, according to the doctrine, separate institutions should exercise these powers.
  Montesquieu was greatly influenced in his account of the separation of powers by his observation of the post-1688 British constitution. Twentieth century critics have argued that British constitutional practice does not in fact reflect any thoroughgoing separation of powers, and indeed never did. It is true that Montesquieu failed to remark the emergence of the Cabinet system—our parliamentary executive—and the difficulties this would create for a "pure" rendering of the separation of powers. But Montesquieu did not, in fairness, insist on an absolute division of the functions of the state between separate institutions. This is evident from his acceptance of the need for "checks and balances". This term refers to means by which the institutions of the state could influence and restrict each other's actions, and would seem to imply some scope for one institution trespassing in the sphere of one or both of the others. In any case, twentieth century "trashing" of the separation of powers doctrine "does not do justice to the contribution

which the doctrine has made to the maintenance of liberty and the continuing need by constitutional means to restrain abuse of governmental power" (Bradley and Ewing, 1997).

In descriptive terms, nevertheless, there is at first glance much to support the view that the separation of powers is not a feature of the British constitution. There are obvious institutional overlaps. The Sovereign, in a formal sense, is part of the legislature, executive and judiciary, as is the Lord Chancellor in a rather more practical sense. The government is drawn from Parliament. But while there may be some crossover in terms of personnel, are functional divisions nevertheless observed?

The primary legislative function is vested in the Queen in Parliament. Yet certain autonomous powers of the Crown to legislate by Order in Council survived the 1688 settlement. Legislative powers are frequently delegated by Parliament to executive bodies such as ministers and local authorities, even to the extent of authorising ministers to amend or repeal primary legislation. In matters of E.C. law, the Council of Ministers and European Commission legislate for the United Kingdom. And in a more basic sense, it may be said that the primary legislative function is only formally vested in the Queen in Parliament. Government bills dominate that part of parliamentary time devoted to the legislative process and no other bills will be passed without government support. If the government has a working Commons majority, it is very exceptional for its legislation to be rejected by the Commons. The powers of the House of Lords to amend legislation passed by the Commons are limited, and its consent may be dispensed with anyway under the Parliament Acts. By convention, the Queen never refuses the Royal Assent. In an *effective* sense, then, it might be more accurate to say that the primary legislative function is at the disposal of the government of the day.

The executive function is residual, comprising anything which is not clearly legislative or judicial. Yet the executive does possess legislative and judicial powers as well. The relationship of executive and legislature we have noted. The relationship of executive and judiciary is a little more subtle. By and large, the executive does not seek to exercise essential judicial functions, such as the conduct of trials, although it has run into trouble before the European Court of Human Rights for assuming powers which, under the European Convention, should be subject to judicial decision (*e.g. X v. U.K.* (1981)). In the past, moreover, as the state assumed increasing powers in the areas of economic regulation and social welfare, it was often decided to entrust disputes arising out of new statutory schemes not to the ordinary courts but to ministers directly, or to administrative tribunals. The functions of these executive bodies were, at least, "quasi-judicial". In time, this process gave rise to concern and the government appointed a Committee on Administrative Tribunals and Inquiries under the chairmanship of Sir Oliver Franks. The Report of the Franks Committee in 1957, which led to legislation, established a number of important principles applicable to "administrative justice" of this sort, among them the independence of administrative tribunals from the government department concerned with their work, and the application of truly judicial standards of openness, fairness and impartiality to their procedures. There may be sensible reasons for entrusting particular disputes to tribunals, but the Franks Report made clear that where this is done, such bodies are to be regarded as part of the machinery of justice and must act accordingly.

Do the courts exercise legislative functions; and does Parliament exercise judicial functions? The involvement of the Lord Chancellor and Lords of Appeal in Ordinary in the legislative business of the House of Lords is far less significant than the role of the judiciary in interpreting legislation and in applying and developing the common law. Judges do not like the term "judicial legislation" but sometimes it is not inapposite. By contrast, Parliament exercises only a limited judicial function in relation to the enforcement of its privileges and punishment of breaches of privilege.

But it is misleading to concentrate exclusively on how far our constitutional arrangements mirror a pure theory of the separation of powers when assessing the validity of the doctrine in the United Kingdom. The separation of powers is not only a descriptive doctrine. It is prescriptive too: it says what *should* happen if the monopolisation of state power is to be avoided. That is the motivating force behind the doctrine, and it is perhaps more instructive to look for instances of inter-institutional tension—checks and balances—which may be positively enhanced by departures from an over-rigid separation of powers. So, for example, the fact that the government is drawn from Parliament and is responsible to it enables the legislature to scrutinise, criticise and sometimes even oust the government (although how far and how well Parliament actually does any of these things is questionable). The Franks Report, mentioned above, may be seen as a powerful vindication of the continuing relevance of the reasoning which underpins the separation of powers doctrine. Perhaps the most important and systematic check and balance in modern times is judicial review of administrative action. Since the 1960s, enormous advances have been made in this field. This was a vital, if belated, response to the great expansion in the power of the executive in the first half of the twentieth century; today, the supervisory jurisdiction of the courts is deployed with impressive intensity to ensure that the powers of the executive are exercised within their legal limits and in accordance with judge-made principles of good administration. The courts do not have the power to review the validity of primary legislation, but even here the winds of change have been and will continue to be felt: an Act of Parliament incompatible with E.C. law may be disapplied by the courts, and the courts will have jurisdiction under the Human Rights Act 1998 (once enacted) to declare an Act of Parliament incompatible with the rights therein enshrined.

It is fitting to conclude this chapter with reference to judicial review, for it is clear that the courts could not perform this vital aspect of the judicial function if subjected to undue interference by either the executive or the legislature. The British version of the separation of powers may be messy and imperfect, but it does recognise the fundamental importance of judicial independence, which is necessary not only in separation of powers terms but also for the maintenance of the rule of law and constitutional government in general.

8. THE EUROPEAN CONVENTION ON HUMAN RIGHTS

INTRODUCTION

The European Convention on Human Rights is a product of the Council of Europe, which was established during the post-war period of reconciliation and reconstruction in 1949. The Convention was signed at Rome in 1950, ratified by the United Kingdom in 1951, and it entered into force in 1953. It is to be incorporated into the domestic legal systems of the United Kingdom in 1998.

For the time being, however, the rights enshrined in the Convention and its protocols cannot be relied on and enforced directly in United Kingdom courts. In the United Kingdom, the signing and ratifying of international treaties are prerogative acts of the Crown; consequently, treaties have no domestic legal force unless and until incorporated by Act of Parliament. The English courts adopt a presumption, when construing a statute, that Parliament does not intend to infringe the international obligations of the United Kingdom: therefore, in cases where a statute is ambiguous or open to two competing interpretations, the English courts will construe the legislation so as to achieve consistency with the Convention. The Scottish courts, by contrast, rejected this approach in the past: *Kaur v. Lord Advocate* (1980); *Moore v. Secretary of State for Scotland* (1985). However, in *T, Petitioner* (1996) the Court of Session departed from its former approach and adopted that followed in England. But in both Scotland and England, where the meaning of an Act of Parliament is clear, the courts must give effect to it, however much that may contravene the Convention. The individual's remedy will then lie in a petition to the European Commission and Court of Human Rights in Strasbourg.

THE SCOPE OF THE EUROPEAN CONVENTION ON HUMAN RIGHTS

The United Kingdom is obliged by Article 1 of the Convention to protect the rights laid down therein. These rights include: the right to life (Article 2); freedom from torture or inhuman or degrading treatment or punishment (Article 3); freedom from slavery or servitude (Article 4); the right to liberty and security of one's person (Article 5); the right to a fair trial (Article 6); freedom from retroactive criminal convictions or penalties (Article 7); the right to respect for one's private and family life, home and correspondence (Article 8); freedom of thought, conscience and religion (Article 9); freedom of expression (Article 10); freedom of assembly and association (Article 11); and the right to marry and found a family (Article 12). An effective remedy before a national authority must be secured to those whose rights and freedoms as set forth in the Convention have been violated (Article 13). And under Article 14, the enjoyment of the rights and freedoms enshrined in the Convention must be secured to all without any discrimination on any grounds such as sex, race, colour, language, religion, political or other opinion, national or social origin, association with a national minority, property, birth or other status. Since 1950, the Convention has been supplemented several times by the addition of Protocols, such as the First Protocol signed at Paris in 1952. This enshrines the right to the peaceful enjoyment of one's possessions, the right to education and the right to take part in regular free elections held by secret ballot.

None of the Convention articles is absolute. Even the right to life may be infringed "in the execution of a sentence of a court following ... conviction of a crime for which [the death] penalty is provided by law" and "when it results from the use of force which is no more than absolutely necessary: a) in defence of any person from unlawful violence; b) in order to effect a lawful arrest or to prevent the escape of a person lawfully detained; c) in action lawfully taken for the purpose of quelling a riot or insurrection". Articles 8–11 may be subject to limitations which are prescribed by law and which are necessary in a democratic society in the interests of such factors as national security, the protection of public order or the prevention of disorder and crime, the protection of public health, safety or morals, the protection of the rights and freedoms of others and the prevention of disclosure of confidential information. Moreover, a state may derogate under Article 15 from its obligations under the Convention in time of war or other public emergency threatening the life of the nation, to the extent strictly required by the exigencies of the situation. Only Article 2 (except in respect of deaths resulting from lawful acts of war), Article 3, Article 4(1) and Article 7 are non-derogable. The United Kingdom entered a derogation from Article 5(3) (which requires that persons arrested or detained shall be brought promptly before a judge) after the European Court of Human Rights held in *Brogan v. U.K.* (1988) that there had been a violation of Article 5(3) in detaining suspected terrorists under section 12 of the Prevention of Terrorism (Temporary Provisions) Act 1984 for four days and six hours.

THE PROCEDURE OF THE EUROPEAN COURT OF HUMAN RIGHTS

An individual who complains of a violation of his rights under the Convention directs his complaint in the first instance to the European Commission of Human Rights. The Commission must decide whether the complaint is admissible, *i.e.* compatible with the Convention, not manifestly ill-founded and not an abuse of process. The complainant must also have exhausted all available domestic remedies and must have raised his petition within the prescribed six-month time-limit. If the petition is accepted (most are not), the Commission itself investigates the complaint and attempts to broker a friendly settlement. Failing that, the Commission reports on the dispute to the state concerned and to the Committee of Ministers of the Council of Europe.

The Committee of Ministers itself, acting by two-thirds majority, decides whether there has been a violation of the Convention if within three months the case is not referred to the Court of Human Rights. References to the Court may only be made by the Commission or by the state concerned, and only if the state concerned has accepted the compulsory jurisdiction of the Court or has consented to it in the particular instance. The decision of the Court is final, and it has power, if available national remedies are insufficient, to "afford just satisfaction" to the victim of a violation, including the award of damages against the state.

It is not only individuals who may complain to Strasbourg of a violation of the Convention. Under Article 24, any state party to the Convention may refer to the Commission any alleged breach of the Convention by another state party. There have been very few inter-state references by comparison to the number of petitions raised by individuals. In *Ireland v. U.K.* (1978), however, the Court held the United Kingdom to be in breach of Article 3 in its use in the early 1970s of interrogation techniques involving hooding, standing detainees against walls for prolonged periods, subjection to continuous and monotonous noise, deprivation of sleep and deprivation of food and drink in respect of suspected terrorists.

These procedures will change comprehensively with the entry into force of Protocol 11 to the Convention in November 1998. Protocol 11 replaces Parts II to IV of the Convention, and the Second Protocol, with a new Part II which establishes a permanent court. The new court will assume the jurisdiction presently held by the Court and Commission; the filtering role of the Commission will thus be removed. The court will be staffed by judges appointed from each of the states party to the Convention, and will carry out its work at four different levels. A committee of the court, consisting of three judges, may by unanimous vote declare inadmissible an application submitted to the court: Article 28. This decision is final. A Chamber consisting of seven judges must decide on the admissibility and merits of individual applications if no decision is taken under Article 28; and shall decide on the admissibility and merits of inter-state applications. The judge representing the "defendant" state must be a member of the Chamber hearing the case against the state. Appeals (by any party to a case, including individual applicants) lie from a decision of a Chamber to the Grand Chamber, consisting of 17 judges, under Article 43. A Chamber may choose, furthermore, to relinquish jurisdiction in favour of the Grand Chamber where a case raises a serious question affecting the interpretation of the Convention or where the resolution of the case by the Chamber might conflict with a judgment previously given by the Court: Article 30. Finally, the plenary court is charged by Article 26 with electing the President and Vice-President(s) of the Court, setting up the Chambers and electing Presidents of the Chambers, adopting the rules of the Court and electing the Registrar and Deputy Registrar(s).

THE UNITED KINGDOM BEFORE THE COURT OF HUMAN RIGHTS

The United Kingdom granted the right of individual petition in 1966 and has since renewed it every five years. The first case involving the United

Kingdom to reach the Court (bearing in mind that most cases, if not rejected as inadmissible, are settled by the Commission) was *Golder v. U.K.* (1975), in which it was held that the refusal by prison authorities to grant a convicted prisoner access to legal advice was in breach of Article 8 (respect for private life and correspondence) and Article 6(1) (in that a right of access to legal advice is an aspect of the right to a fair trial). The fight against terrorism in Northern Ireland has accounted for a significant proportion of the cases brought against the United Kingdom, among them *Ireland v. U.K.* (1978), *Brogan v. U.K.* (1988) and *McCann v. U.K.* (1996).

Campbell and Cosans v. U.K.* (1980) is the only Scottish case to have made its way to the Court. There, two mothers complained that the use of the tawse in Scottish schools was a violation of Article 3, as a form of inhuman or degrading punishment; and of Article 2 of the First Protocol, which provides that in the provision of education and teaching the state must respect the right of parents to ensure that their children are educated in conformity with their religious and philosophical convictions. The Court rejected the first of these arguments but accepted the second on the grounds that "philosophical convictions" denotes "such convictions as are worthy of respect in a 'democratic society' ... and are not incompatible with human dignity; ... [and which do] not conflict with the fundamental right of the child to education". It was held that the provision of efficient instruction and training and the avoidance of unreasonable expenditure, which the United Kingdom had pleaded in its defence, was not incompatible with a system of exemption for individual pupils from a system of corporal punishment. In fact, it was provided in the Education (No. 2) Act 1986 that corporal punishment in all state schools in the United Kingdom was to be abolished. Again in *Costello-Roberts v. U.K.* (1995) the Court held that the use of corporal punishment against a seven-year-old boy in a private boarding school did not, on the facts, constitute a violation of Article 3.

Space precludes a detailed consideration of the cases in which the United Kingdom has been involved, but note, among the more important decisions of the Court, *Sunday Times v. U.K.* (1979), which held that the law of contempt of court in relation to publications as stated by the House of Lords in *Att.-Gen. v. Times Newspapers* (1974) was in breach of Article 10 of the Convention; *Dudgeon v. U.K.* (1981), which held that legislation in Northern Ireland which criminalised homosexual activities between consenting adult males was in breach of Article 8; *Malone v. U.K.* (1984), which held that Article 8 had been violated by telephone tapping without positive legal authorisation; and *Observer and Guardian v. U.K.* (1991), which held that the continuance in force of interim injunctions prohibiting press coverage of the allegations of malpractice made in *Spycatcher*, even though the book had been published widely elsewhere in the world, was in breach of Article 10.

Where an adverse judgment is given against it, the United Kingdom comes under an international legal obligation to change national law so as to conform with the Convention (unless it enters a derogation). The approach to compliance has on occasion been somewhat grudging. The provisions of the Contempt of Court Act 1981, enacted in the light of the *Sunday Times* decision, do the bare minimum necessary to achieve compliance; and indeed the United Kingdom was in trouble again in *Goodwin v. U.K.* (1996) in respect of the conviction of a journalist for contempt after he refused to reveal his sources. Similarly, after it was held in *Abdulaziz v. U.K.* (1985) that British immigration rules discriminated against women contrary to Articles 8 and 14 in that, while the wives and fiancées of men permanently settled in the United Kingdom were entitled to enter the United Kingdom the husbands and fiancés of women were not, the discrimination was eradicated by removing the entitlement of wives and fiancées to enter: levelling down rather than levelling up.

INCORPORATION OF THE CONVENTION

The Human Rights Bill was introduced in the House of Lords in November 1997 and at time of writing is making its way through Parliament. Clause 1 of and Schedule 1 to the bill specify those Articles of the Convention and the First Protocol which are to be incorporated. Clause 2 provides that a court or tribunal determining a question in connection with a Convention right must have regard to the relevant judgments, decisions, declarations and opinions of the European Commission and Court of Human Rights and the Committee of Ministers of the Council of Europe. *All* courts and tribunals shall also, in construing primary and subordinate legislation *passed or to be passed*, read and give effect to it, so far as possible, consistently with the Convention rights (although this will have no effect on the validity, continuing operation or enforcement of any legislation which cannot be so construed): clause 3. Only certain specified courts, however, will have jurisdiction to make a "declaration of incompatibility" in respect of primary or subordinate legislation which cannot be construed to achieve consistency with Convention rights, namely (for Scotland) the House of Lords, the Judicial Committee of the Privy Council, the Courts-Martial Appeal Court, the High Court of Justiciary sitting as a court of criminal appeal and the Court of Session: clause 4(5). Again, it is expressly provided that a declaration of incompatibility will have no effect on the validity, continuing operation or enforcement of the provision in respect of which it is given; nor is it binding on the parties to the proceedings in which it is made: clause 4(6). This seeks to preserve, at least in appearance, parliamentary supremacy: theoretically, it will remain open to Parliament to ignore a declaration of incompatibility, and such a declaration is *not* to be regarded as a binding decision that the Act of Parliament in question is *ultra vires* and invalid.

However, clause 10 of the bill lays down powers to take "remedial action". If a provision of legislation has been declared to be incompatible with Convention rights, or if it appears to a minister of the Crown or Her Majesty in Council that, in the light of a finding of the European Court of Human Rights, a provision of legislation is incompatible with obligations of the United Kingdom arising from the Convention, the minister may by order make such amendments to the legislation (including its repeal) as he considers appropriate. Such a remedial order must be approved in draft by resolution of each House of Parliament except where urgency requires that the order is made without a draft being approved, in which case this must be stated expressly in the order and the order must be laid before Parliament after it is made. Each House must approve the order within 40 days or it will cease to have effect. Moreover, clause 19 of the bill seeks to avoid declarations of incompatibility by providing that a minister in charge of a bill in either House of Parliament must, before second reading of the bill, make a statement to the effect that in his view the provisions of the bill are compatible with the Convention rights. If he is unable so to do, he must state that the government nevertheless wishes the House to proceed with the bill. In either case, the statement must be in writing and be published in such manner as the minister considers appropriate.

Clause 6 provides that public authorities may not lawfully act in a way which is incompatible with one or more of the Convention rights, unless the authority was unable to act differently as a result of provisions of primary or subordinate legislation which cannot be construed and given effect in a manner compatible with the Convention rights. The term "public authority" is defined to include a court or tribunal and "any person certain of whose functions are functions of a public nature", but *not* either House of Parliament (other than the House of Lords in its judicial capacity) or anyone exercising functions in connection with proceedings in Parliament. A person who claims that a public authority has acted or proposes to act in a way which is unlawful in terms of clause 6 may, if and only if he is or would be a victim of such unlawful act, bring proceedings against the authority in the appropriate court or tribunal or rely on the Convention right or rights concerned in any legal proceedings: clause 7. The court or tribunal seised of such a dispute may "grant such relief or remedy, or make such order, within its jurisdiction as it considers just and appropriate", including damages. Damages may only be awarded, however, by a court which has power to award damages or to order payment of compensation in civil proceedings, and no award of damages may be made unless the court is satisfied, having regard to all the circumstances, that the award is necessary to afford just satisfaction to the person in whose favour it is made: clause 8.

In comparing the provisions of the Human Rights Bill with the provisions of the Scotland Bill on devolution, it will be noted that the emphasis in both is that the legislative supremacy of the Westminster Parliament is unaffected by their provisions. The government appears to be seeking to achieve far-reaching measures of constitutional reform while at the same time keeping faith with the British constitutional tradition, of which parliamentary supremacy is very much a part. A parallel may also be drawn between the power conferred on the courts by the Human Rights Bill to make "declarations of incompatibility" with the role of the courts in relation to E.C. law. We have seen that the courts will declare an Act of Parliament to be incompatible with E.C. law: *R. v. Transport Secretary, ex parte Factortame (No. 2)* (1991); *R. v. Employment Secretary, ex parte Equal Opportunities Commission* (1995). What the courts do *not* do, however, is hold such an Act to be *ultra vires* and void for incompatibility with E.C. law. Their language is of "compatibility" rather than "validity"—consciously so—and their judgments are to that extent advisory rather than dispositive. Thus it falls to Parliament to correct the incompatibility that the courts have declared if it sees fit to do so, and although in practice it has always done so, this approach preserves at least a veneer of legal truth in the notion that Parliament can make or unmake any law whatever and no court may set aside an Act of Parliament.

9. POLICE POWERS

ARREST

Arrests are almost always made by police officers. The power of ordinary people to effect a "citizen's arrest" is strictly circumscribed in Scotland. It was held in *Codona v. Cardle* (1989) and *Bryans v. Guild* (1990) that the law is as stated in Renton and Brown's *Criminal Procedure*: "A private citizen is entitled to arrest without warrant for a serious crime he has witnessed, or perhaps where, being the victim of the crime, he has information equivalent to personal observation, as where the fleeing criminal is pointed out to him by an eye-witness." Beyond this, a private citizen who purports to arrest a person may render himself liable to conviction for assault.

The meaning of arrest was considered in *Forbes v. H.M. Advocate* (1990). For an arrest to be lawful, the High Court of Justiciary stressed that the police should make clear to the arrestee that he is under legal compulsion and should tell him the (correct) reason for his arrest. It is preferable to use the word "arrest" here, but "any form of words will suffice to inform the person that he is being arrested if they bring to his notice the fact that he is under compulsion and the person thereafter submits to that compulsion" (*per* Lord Parker C.J. in *Alderson v. Booth* (1969)). Reasonable physical force may be used to effect an arrest, and it is an offence under the Police (Scotland) Act 1967, s. 41, to resist a lawful arrest or to escape from lawful custody.

A person who has been arrested and is in custody has the right, under section 15(1) of the Criminal Procedure (Scotland) Act 1995, to have intimation of his custody and of the place where he is being held sent to a third party without delay, or with no more delay than is necessary in the interest of the investigation or prevention of crime or the apprehension of offenders. He must be informed of this entitlement on arrival at the police station. Under section 17(1) of the 1995 Act, he is also entitled immediately upon arrival to request the attendance of a solicitor at the place where he is being held; again, he must be informed of this right.

Police powers of arrest fall into three categories: arrest with a warrant; arrest without warrant under statutory provisions; and arrest without warrant at common law.

Arrest with a warrant
When an arrest is deemed necessary (because there is sufficient evidence to bring charges), the procurator fiscal will present a petition to the sheriff court or district court seeking the power to arrest the suspect and bring

him before the court (along with other powers such as a power to search the suspect and his property). The sheriff or justice is entitled to grant the warrant without inquiring into the grounds on which it is sought, if he has sworn information that there are reasonable grounds for suspicion. The validity of a warrant may be challenged by way of a bill of suspension in the High Court (*Stuart v. Crowe* (1992)) or, after the trial and in the event of the accused being convicted, by way of a bill or petition to the *nobile officium* of the High Court. A warrant which is valid on its face cannot, however, be challenged in the course of a trial before the sheriff (*Allan v. Tant* (1986)).

Arrest without warrant under statute

A great many statutes confer a power of arrest without warrant on a police constable (usually "in uniform") where certain specified conditions are satisfied. The courts normally require fairly strict compliance by the police with the terms of a statutory power of arrest. In *Wither v. Reid* (1980), the accused was charged with an offence under section 41 of the Police (Scotland) Act 1967 after she resisted a clothing and body search for drugs (none were found), having been arrested under section 24(1) of the Misuse of Drugs Act 1971. Section 24 provides that a constable may arrest without warrant a person whom he reasonably suspects of having committed an offence under the Act if he has reasonable cause to believe that the person will abscond unless arrested, or if he does not know and cannot ascertain the name and address of the person, or if he believes that the name and address given are false. The accused was arrested at Elgin station by police who had received information from her estranged ex-fiancé that she had been to Aberdeen to buy drugs. The sheriff acquitted the accused, holding that there was nothing to justify her arrest under any of the provisions of section 24 and that, as her arrest was illegal, she was entitled to resist the consequently unlawful search. The High Court, by a majority, dismissed the procurator fiscal's appeal.

Note, however, that where (as is usual) a statutory provision makes a power of arrest conditional upon a "reasonable belief" on the part of the arresting officer that an offence has been committed by the arrestee, the courts do not inquire too closely into the reasonableness of the officer's belief or suspicion. It was held in *McLeod v. Shaw* (1981) that the test is subjective: provided the arresting officer honestly believed that the arrestee was committing or had committed the relevant offence, the arrest is valid and lawful unless the officer could have had no reasonable grounds at all for that belief.

Arrest without warrant at common law

It was established in *Peggie v. Clark* (1868) that a constable may at common law arrest without warrant a person whom he reasonably believes to have committed an offence, in order "to prevent justice from being defeated" (*per* Lord Deas).

This translates into a formidably broad power of arrest. Bear in mind that:

- As with arrest without warrant under statute, the reasonableness of the arresting officer's belief that a crime has been committed by the arrestee is assessed subjectively: only if, as in *Cardle v. Murray* (1993), there are no reasonable grounds to support the officer's honest belief will an arrest be unlawful.

- The arrest must be necessary in the interests of justice, as Lord Deas indicated in *Peggie*. It is not enough that an offence has been committed: the arresting officer must also believe, for example, that the person will abscond unless arrested, or will otherwise interfere with the course of justice. Urgency may justify an arrest in the interests of justice; by the same token, the longer the lapse of time since the commission of an offence, the less easy it will be to justify arrest without warrant.

- The more serious the offence concerned, the easier it is to justify arrest without warrant at common law (but note that a constable may arrest without warrant a person who is committing, or who leads the constable reasonably to apprehend, a breach of the peace: *Montgomery v. McLeod* (1977)).

In general terms, as the Lord President put it in *Peggie*, "under special circumstances, a police officer is entitled to apprehend without a warrant, and it will always be a question whether the circumstances justify the apprehension." The only caveat to this proposition is that the circumstances need not be so distinctively "special" as the Lord President perhaps implied.

DETENTION

Statutory powers of "quasi-detention" and detention are now contained in the Criminal Procedure (Scotland) Act 1995, ss. 13 and 14.

Section 13(1)(a) provides that where a constable has reasonable grounds for suspecting that a person has committed or is committing an offence at any place, he may require that person to give his name and address and may ask him for an explanation of the circumstances which have given rise to the constable's suspicion. The constable may require that person to remain with him while he verifies the name and address and/or notes the explanation offered, provided that this can be done quickly, and may use reasonable force to ensure that the person remains with him. The constable must inform the person of his suspicion and of the general nature of the offence which he suspects the person has committed or is committing; and if necessary must inform the person why he is being required to remain with him. He must also inform the person that failure to comply with his requirements may constitute an offence for which he may be arrested without warrant.

Under section 13(1)(b), a constable may also require any other person whom he believes to have information relating to the offence to give his name and address. He must inform that person of the general nature of the offence which he suspects has been or is being committed and that the reason for the requirement is that he believes the person has relevant information. A person who fails to give his name and address without reasonable excuse is guilty of an offence.

Section 14(1) provides that where a constable has reasonable grounds for suspecting that a person has committed or is committing an offence punishable by imprisonment, he may, for the purpose of facilitating the carrying out of investigations into the offence and as to whether criminal proceedings should be instigated against the person, detain that person. Reasonable force may be used. Where a person is detained, the constable may exercise the same powers of search as are available following arrest (see below); again, reasonable force may be used. The detainee must be taken as quickly as is reasonably practicable to a police station or other premises, and may thereafter be taken elsewhere.

Detention must be terminated at the end of six hours, and sooner if it appears that there are no longer grounds for detention or if the detainee is arrested or detained pursuant to another statutory provision. Where a person is released at the termination of a period of detention under section 14(1) he cannot be re-detained under the subsection on the same grounds or on any grounds arising out of the same circumstances. Where a person has previously been detained pursuant to another statutory provision, and is then detained under section 14(1) on the same grounds or on any grounds arising from the same circumstances, the six-hour detention period must be reduced by the length of his earlier detention.

A constable who detains a person under section 14(1) must inform the person of his suspicion, of the general nature of the offence which he suspects has been or is being committed and of the reason for the detention. A number of matters require to be recorded by the police:

- the place where detention begins and the police station or other premises to which the detainee is taken;
- the general nature of the suspected offence;
- the time when detention begins and the time of the detainee's arrival at the police station or other premises;
- the time of the detainee's release from detention or, as the case may be, the time of his arrest;
- that the detainee has been informed of his right, both at the moment of detention and again on arrival at the police station, to refuse to answer any question other than to give his name and address (this is the statutory caution);
- that the detainee has been informed of his rights under section 15(1)(b) of the 1995 Act, namely the right to have intimation of his detention and of the place where he is being held sent to a solicitor and to one other person reasonably named by him (*e.g.* a friend or relative) without delay, or with no more delay than is necessary in the interest of the investigation or prevention of crime or the apprehension of offenders;
- where the detainee exercises his rights under section 15(1)(b), the time at which his request is made and the time at which it is complied with;
- the identity of the constable who informs the detainee of his rights.

An initial point to make about these provisions is that the status of a person required to "remain" under section 13 while a constable checks his name and address and/or notes his explanation is unclear. While the section must mean something less than detention (otherwise there would be no need for section 13 at all), note that a person can not only be required to remain but can be physically constrained to do so. Moreover, while the constable has the power to require an explanation of the circumstances which have given rise to his suspicion, he is not enjoined to administer a caution at this stage. Presumably if the circumstances were such that a constable felt a caution to be appropriate, the section 14 power to detain should be used instead. However, the line between sections 13 and 14—or the line between the situations in which one power or the other is appropriate—is not clear, and it is likely that any explanation offered by a person asked to remain under section 13 would be admissible at a subsequent trial subject to the normal rules of evidence.

So far as detention proper is concerned, it must be stressed that detention is not to be used as a means of delaying arrest and charge. If sufficient evidence emerges to justify arrest of a detainee, detention must be terminated and must in any event be terminated after six hours. Note, however, that in *Grant v. H.M. Advocate* (1990), the accused was not arrested until some 20 minutes after the end of his detention, and objection was taken at his trial to the admissibility in evidence of statements he had made while detained. The High Court held that such lapses in compliance with the strict formalities did not of themselves vitiate what had taken place.

A statutory caution must be administered to the detainee, both at the time of detention and again on arrival at the place of detention. Section 14(7)(a) provides that the power to question a detainee is without prejudice to any relevant rule of law regarding the admissibility in evidence of any answer given. The common law applies a test of fairness to determine issues of admissibility, and it was held in *Tonge, Grey and Jack v. H.M. Advocate* (1982) that a full common law caution should also be administered to a detainee prior to questioning if the evidence thus obtained is to avoid the risk of being held inadmissible because obtained unfairly. Failure to administer the statutory caution is less likely to be fatal to a subsequent prosecution. In *Scott v. Howie* (1993), the accused was detained and taken to the police station. The statutory caution was not given at the moment of detention, but at the commencement of questioning both the statutory caution and a full common law caution were given. The accused then made a statement, which the Crown founded upon at his trial. The High Court held that what had occurred was a procedural defect which did not vitiate the admissibility in evidence of the accused's statement, the statement being open to no objection when measured by the common law test of fairness. Any statements made by the accused between the commencement of his detention and his arrival at the police station would, however, have been inadmissible.

Once detained, the detainee must be removed to a police station or other premises, and during detention he may be removed elsewhere (*e.g.* to take part in an identification parade). In *Menzies v. H.M. Advocate* (1995), the accused was detained near Airdrie and taken to Dunfermline police station, since the interviewing facilities at Airdrie were busy and all the documentation relating to the offence with which the accused was eventually

charged was in Dunfermline. The High Court held that the requirement
that the detainee be taken away "as quickly as is reasonably practicable"
did not mean that he had to be taken to the nearest police station; the
requirement was conditional upon what was reasonably practicable in the
circumstances as they appeared to the constable by whom the person was
detained.

The requirement of recording the details of detention should as a matter
of good police practice be adhered to, although it is arguable that failure to
record a particular detail will not render the detention unlawful and
statements made by the detainee inadmissible. In *Cummings v. H.M.
Advocate* (1982), the only record led in evidence to show that the accused
had received a statutory caution was contained in a police officer's notebook.
This was held to be sufficient.

SEARCH

Search of persons

First, a person may be searched with his or her consent (*Devlin v. Normand*
(1992)). At common law, a person may be searched (and fingerprinted and
photographed) by the police only after arrest, although in situations of
"urgency", searches carried out before arrest may be excused and the
evidence obtained admitted at trial (*Bell v. Hogg* (1967)). Search before
arrest must be justified by reference to some statutory provision, *e.g.* section
23(2) of the Misuse of Drugs Act 1971, whereby a constable who has
reasonable grounds to suspect that a person is in possession of drugs may
detain and search him. On the principle of *Wither v. Reid* (1980), the courts
will normally require the police to comply closely with the terms of statutory
powers of search.

When a person has been arrested and is in custody, or where he has
been detained under section 14 of the Criminal Procedure (Scotland) Act
1995, section 18(2) of that Act provides that a constable may take from that
person fingerprints, palmprints and other such prints and impressions of an
external part of the body as the constable reasonably considers it appropriate
to take, having regard to the circumstances of the suspected offence in respect
of which the person has been arrested or detained. Section 18(6) provides
that the constable may also take, with the authority of an officer of a rank
no lower than inspector, a sample of hair; a sample of fingernail or toenail
(or of material under the nails); a sample of blood or other body fluid, body
tissue or other material from an external part of the body by means of
swabbing or rubbing; or a sample of saliva. Reasonable force may be used.
Section 58 of the Criminal Justice (Scotland) Act 1995 further provides
that swabs may be taken from the mouth for the purpose of DNA
fingerprinting.

If a sample is sought before arrest or detention, or if samples not covered
by the statutory provisions (*e.g.* dental impressions: *Hay v. H.M. Advocate*
(1968)) are required, then the procurator fiscal must seek the authority of a
sheriff's warrant. It was held in *Morris v. MacNeill* (1991) that "such a
warrant will not be lightly granted, and will only be granted where the

circumstances are special and where the granting of the warrant will not disturb the delicate balance that must be maintained between the public interest on the one hand and the interest of the accused on the other". However, it does not appear to require much for the circumstances to be sufficiently special. One factor taken into account here is the seriousness of the offence, yet in *Walker v. Lees* (1995) a warrant was granted to take blood samples from a person suspected of theft from lockfast cars. If the Crown can show that the samples sought will provide useful evidence, they are likely to get the warrant craved: the unusual cases will be those in which the warrant is refused.

Search of premises

It was established in *Bell v. Black and Morrison* (1865) that a general warrant to search any premises for any articles is incompetent. A search warrant must be specific in its terms and the police must keep within the limits of a warrant when conducting a search under it: a police officer authorised by warrant to search for article X may not actively look for article Y. As this implies, the officers who conduct a search must be aware of the specifications of the warrant. The officers were not so aware in *Leckie v. Miln* (1981). In their search of the suspect's house, they removed a number of articles which were outside the terms of the warrant. These articles were held by the High Court to have been unlawfully obtained. They were therefore inadmissible in evidence against the accused and his conviction for theft was quashed. Nor did it matter that the police had been given permission to search the house by the suspect's wife: any permission must be treated as limited to a search conducted within the terms of the warrant.

It often happens, however, that police officers engaged on a lawful search of premises stumble across articles not covered by the warrant. Can such articles lawfully be removed, and will they be admissible in evidence? In *H.M. Advocate v. Hepper* (1958), Lord Guthrie held that "the police officers were not prevented from taking possession of other articles of a plainly incriminatory character which they happened to come across in the course of their search." In *Drummond v. H.M. Advocate* (1992), the accused was charged with the theft of clothes. Some of the clothes had been found in a wardrobe at his home as it was searched by two police officers executing a warrant relating to stolen furniture. When the first constable was asked what he was looking for in the wardrobe, he admitted that he was looking for "stuff" from the clothing theft. The sheriff ruled his evidence inadmissible. The second constable, however, said that he had a list of the stolen furniture which included small items such as lamps, and that he was looking for these items in the wardrobe when the stolen clothing attracted his attention. The sheriff allowed the evidence of the second constable to go to the jury, which convicted the accused.

At common law, the power of the police to enter and search private premises is limited. As a starting point, it may be said that the right of a police officer to enter private premises for any purpose without a warrant and without the occupier's consent is no greater than that of any other member of the public; and if the police do so enter, they must be prepared to justify their conduct by reference to special circumstances before any evidence thus obtained may be held admissible (*Cairns v. Keane* (1983)). As the Lord Justice-General put it in *Lawrie v. Muir* (1950):

"Irregularities require to be excused, and infringements of the formalities of the law in relation to these matters are not lightly to be condoned. Whether any given irregularity ought to be excused depends upon the nature of the irregularity and the circumstances under which it was committed."

An urgent need to obtain evidence, particularly in relation to serious offences, may justify a search without warrant of private property (*H.M. Advocate v. McGuigan* (1936)). Other circumstances which may excuse an irrregular search are the authority and good faith of those who obtained the evidence. In *Lawrie v. Muir*, one ground upon which the High Court quashed the conviction was that the evidence had been obtained from the accused's dairy not by police officers but by two inspectors who should have known "the precise limits of their authority and should be held to exceed these limits at their peril." Similarly, in relation to search of a person rather than search of premises, it was held in *Wilson v. Brown* (1996) that stewards employed at Hangar 13 in Ayr could legitimately have detained the accused until the police arrived, but that they had no authority whatsoever to search him (finding, in the process, 78 temazepam capsules) and that the circumstances were not such as to excuse the irregularity of the search. Good faith was a factor in *Webley v. Ritchie* (1997). There, the accused was convicted of the theft of three squash racquets. While he was in detention in connection with the theft, two police officers located his car, forced it open and found the stolen racquets in the boot. The racquets were held to be admissible in evidence at his trial, not only because the police had acted reasonably and in good faith in forcing open the car, but also because, as there was a risk that the six-hour detention period would expire before a warrant could be obtained, there was an urgent need to search the car in order to preserve any evidence. The offence, however, can hardly be described as "serious".

Overarching all of these factors is the general principle governing the admissibility of evidence, namely the test of fairness. This is considered further in the next section.

QUESTIONING

Once a person has been formally charged, he cannot be questioned further about the offence with which he has been charged (*Carmichael v. Boyd* (1993)). But there is no general rule that the police cannot question a person after he has been arrested, provided the questioning is not unfair (*Johnston v. H.M. Advocate* (1993)), and of course questioning is often the very point of detention under section 14 of the Criminal Procedure (Scotland) Act 1995.

An important aspect of the fairness of questioning, and hence of the admissibility in evidence of statements made in response, is cautioning the person being questioned. We have seen, in the context of detention, that the police should administer a statutory caution to the detainee both at the moment of detention and again on arrival at the police station; and a full common law caution should also be given prior to questioning a detainee (*Tonge, Grey and Jack v. H.M. Advocate* (1982)). To avoid any risk of rendering statements inadmissible, a common law caution should be administered at the outset of any form of questioning, and readministered as often as necessary during a long period of questioning: the suspect should be told that he is not obliged to say anything, but that anything he does say will be taken down (and tape-recorded) and may be used in evidence. But there is no absolute rule that a caution must always be given. In *Pennycuick v. Lees* (1992), where the accused was charged with benefits fraud, objection was taken to the admissibility of incriminating statements made by the accused in response to questions from social security investigators on the grounds that the investigators had failed to caution him. The Lord Justice-General held:

"There is ... no rule of law which requires that a suspect must always be cautioned before any question can be put to him by the police or by anyone else by whom the inquiries are being conducted. The question in each case is whether what was done was unfair to the accused. ... [I]t is important to note that there is no suggestion in [this] case that any undue pressure, deception or other device was used to obtain the admissions."

In *Young v. Friel* (1992) it was argued unsuccessfully that the police officer had unfairly induced the accused to make self-incriminating statements when he told the accused that "I can't offer you any deals at present". However, in *H.M. Advocate v. Graham* (1991) it was held that incriminating statements made by the accused to a business colleague and secretly recorded by the police with the colleague's knowledge were inadmissible in evidence. In short, then, failure to caution is not fatal to the admissibility of statements given in response to questioning, provided that there is no suggestion of inducement, entrapment, deception, pressure or anything else apt to render the questioning unfair.

A trial judge will normally be justified in withholding the evidence of statements from the jury only if he is satisfied that no reasonable jury could hold that the evidence had not been extracted from the suspect by unfair or improper means—in other words, only if "it is abundantly clear that the rules of fairness and fair dealing have been flagrantly transgressed" (*per* Lord Cameron in *H.M. Advocate v. Whitelaw* (1980); and see also *Lord Advocate's Reference (No. 1 of 1983)* (1984)). But what exactly the rules of fairness require is not necessarily easy to pin down. A position relatively favourable to the accused was adopted in *Chalmers v. H.M. Advocate* (1954). The Lord Justice-General held:

"by our law, self-incriminating statements when tendered in evidence at a criminal trial, are always jealously examined from the standpoint of being assured as to their spontaneity; and if, on a review of all the proved circumstances, that test is not satisfied, evidence of such statements will usually be excluded altogether."

Subsequently, in *Miln v. Cullen* (1967), the High Court shifted the emphasis of the test of fairness further in the direction of the public interest in the detection and prosecution of crime. The Lord Justice-Clerk observed that:

"While, according to our common law, no man is bound to incriminate himself, there is, in general, nothing to prevent a man making a voluntary and incriminating statement to the police if he so chooses, and evidence being led of that statement at his subsequent trial on the charge to which the statement relates. ... [In this case] there was no interrogation in the proper sense of that word, no extraction of a confession by cross-examination, no taint of undue pressure, cajoling or trapping, no bullying and nothing in the nature of third degree, and it is not suggested that the respondent, by reason of low intelligence, immaturity or drink, was incapable of appreciating what was going on."

More recent cases, however, may indicate a shift back towards *Chalmers*. In *Black v. Annan* (1995) Lord Sutherland held that:

"If the question of impropriety is raised, it lies with the Crown to establish that any statement was in fact voluntarily made and that there was no unfairness in the extraction of that statement. It is not a matter of the accused having to establish that there was sufficient impropriety to justify the extraction of the statement made by him."

In *Codona v. H.M. Advocate* (1996), a 14-year-old girl had been convicted along with three young men of murder. Her conviction was quashed on the grounds that the evidence of her statements in response to police questioning should not have been allowed to go to the jury. The questioning had taken place over some three and a half hours and was of such a character as to demonstrate an intention to extract admissions which the girl was unwilling to make voluntarily. This, coupled with the girl's age and vulnerability (her damaging admissions were only made at a late stage of the questioning, after she had begun to cry), was sufficient to render what had happened unfair. But *Codona* should not necessarily be taken as confined to its special circumstances. In general terms, the Lord Justice-General held that:

"in order that a statement made by an accused person to the police may be available as evidence against him, it must be truly spontaneous and voluntary. The police may question a suspect, but when they move into the field of cross-examination or interrogation, they move into an area of great difficulty. If the questioning is carried too far, by means of leading or repetitive questioning or by pressure in other ways in an effort to obtain from the suspect what they are seeking to obtain from him, the statement is likely to be excluded on the ground that it was extracted by unfair means. Lord Justice-General Emslie's definition of the words 'interrogation' and 'cross-examination' in *Lord Advocate's Reference (No. 1 of 1983)*, as referring only to improper forms of questioning tainted with an element of bullying or pressure designed to break the will of the suspect or to force from him a confession against his will, should not be understood as implying any weakening of these important principles."

Although, as Sheriff Gordon remarks in his commentary on *Codona*, the issue of whether police questioning "degenerated into unacceptable pressure might be regarded as quintessentially one for the jury", the stricter the test of fairness then the easier it is for a trial judge to justify withholding evidence from the jury on the basis that no reasonable jury could conclude that it had been fairly obtained.

---

10. PUBLIC ORDER

Freedom of assembly is enshrined as a fundamental right in Article 11 of the European Convention. As a matter of Scots law, however, there is no legal right to assemble, protest and demonstrate: "you may say what you like ... but that does not mean you may say it anywhere" (*per* Lord Dunedin in *McAra v. Magistrates of Edinburgh* (1913)). One is only free to assemble within the restrictions imposed by the law, and both common law and statute contain an impressive array of powers to maintain and enforce public order.

STATUTORY CONTROLS ON PUBLIC PROCESSIONS

Section 62 of the Civic Government (Scotland) Act 1982 ("the 1982 Act") lays down a general requirement of advance notification of public processions. Note, however, that:

- Advance notification is not required for processions which are "customarily or commonly held" (unless the local authority has disapplied this exemption from certain customary processions; the authority may also exempt certain processions from the requirement of advance notification even though they do not fall into the "customarily or commonly held" class).
- The local authority may waive the full period of notice but not the requirement of notification as such in respect of processions which are spontaneous or organised urgently in response to a particular event and

which cannot therefore be notified in advance in accordance with section 62.

In general, then, the organisers of a public procession must give the relevant local authority and chief constable at least seven days' notice of the procession. Under section 63 of the 1982 Act, the council may, after consulting the chief constable, issue an order either prohibiting the procession or imposing upon it conditions as to its date, time, duration and route. The council may also prohibit entry by the procession into any public place specified in the order. The order must be issued in writing at least two days before the procession is, or was to be, held.

Under section 64, appeals lie to the sheriff against an order made under section 63 within 14 days of receipt of the order. The sheriff may only uphold an appeal if he considers that the council in arriving at its decision to make the order erred in law, based itself on a material error of fact, exercised its discretion unreasonably (in the *Wednesbury* sense) or otherwise acted beyond its powers. These grounds do not provide very exacting controls on the wide discretion possessed by local authorities under section 63.

Section 65 provides that it is an offence to hold a procession without giving notice as required by section 62 or in contravention of the terms of an order made under section 63. A person who takes part in such a procession and who refuses to desist when required to do so by a uniformed police officer is also guilty of an offence.

The 1982 Act only provided for advance control of processions by local authorities. It did not confer on the police powers to impose conditions, which powers may have proved necessary in the event of unforeseen developments during a march. Section 12 of the Public Order Act 1986 was therefore extended to Scotland. Under this provision, the senior police officer present at the scene of any public procession may impose conditions as to time, place and manner where, having regard to the time, place, circumstances and route in or on which any public procession is being held, he reasonably believes that it may lead to serious public disorder, serious damage to property or serious disruption of the life of the community; or that the purpose of the organisers is to intimidate others with a view to preventing them doing what they have a right to do or compelling them to do something that they have no right to do. The conditions imposed must be those that the police officer believes to be necessary to prevent serious disorder, damage to property, disruption or intimidation. The senior police officer may likewise impose conditions in advance of a procession, but only where people are assembling with a view to taking part in it. The "senior police officer" is the officer most senior in rank present at the scene. Under section 12(4) and (5) it is an offence knowingly to fail to comply with conditions imposed under this section, although it is a defence to prove that the failure arose from circumstances beyond one's control. It is also an offence under section 12(6) to incite others to commit an offence under this section.

STATUTORY CONTROLS ON PUBLIC ASSEMBLIES

Powers to regulate and control public assemblies are conferred directly upon the police by section 14 of the Public Order Act 1986 ("the 1986 Act"). If the senior police officer, having regard to the time, place and circumstances in which any public assembly is being or is intended to be held, reasonably believes that it may lead to serious public disorder, serious damage to property or serious disruption of the life of the community, or that the purpose of the organisers is intimidatory in the sense described above, he may give directions imposing on the organisers and participants such conditions as to the venue, duration and maximum number of persons who may take part as appear necessary to prevent such serious disorder, damage or disruption.

These powers apply to a "public assembly", which is defined by section 16 of the Act as meaning "an assembly of 20 or more persons in a public place which is wholly or partly open to the air". "Public place" means "any road within the meaning of the Roads (Scotland) Act 1984" and "any place to which at the material time the public or any section of the public has access, on payment or otherwise, as of right or by virtue of express or implied permission". Where an assembly is in progress, the "senior police officer" is the officer most senior in rank present at the scene. Where an assembly has been proposed, it is the chief officer of police, whose directions must be issued in writing.

A person who organises or takes part in such an assembly and who knowingly fails to comply with such directions is guilty of an offence (section 14(4) and (5)) although it is a defence in either case to prove that failure to comply was due to circumstances beyond one's control. It is also an offence to incite others to commit an offence under this section (section 14(6)).

These powers are clearly limited by the wording of the statute: the police cannot impose conditions on either processions or assemblies unless serious consequences are anticipated. But these powers are not to be taken in isolation. Moreover, the statutory powers of the police in relation to assemblies were augmented by the Criminal Justice and Public Order Act 1994 ("the 1994 Act"). Section 70 of that Act inserted new sections 14A and 14B into the Public Order Act 1986. Section 14A prohibits "trespassory assemblies", meaning an assembly of 20 or more persons on land wholly in the open air (here, partly in the open air is not enough) to which the public has no or only limited right of access. If at any time the chief officer of police reasonably believes that a trespassory assembly is intended to be held and that it is likely to cause serious disruption to the life of the community or significant damage to the land or a building or monument on it (where the land, building or monument are of historical, architectural, archaeological or scientific importance), he may apply to the local authority for an order prohibiting for a specified period not exceeding four days all trespassory assemblies in an area not exceeding the area represented by a circle with a radius of five miles from a specified centre.

Section 14B prescribes the offences in connection with trespassory assemblies. A person who organises or takes part in an assembly which he knows to be prohibited by an order made under section 14A is guilty of an offence. A person who incites others to take part in a prohibited assembly is also guilty of an offence.

Section 71 of the 1994 Act inserted a new section 14C into the 1986 Act. This gives a uniformed police officer the power to stop a person whom he reasonably believes to be on his way to an assembly prohibited by an order made under section 14A and to direct that person not to proceed in the direction of the assembly. This power is only exercisable within the area covered by the order. Failure to comply with the police officer's direction is an offence.

Further powers created by the Criminal Justice and Public Order Act 1994 were criticised as a form of "lifestyle censorship". Sections 61 and 62 confer powers to remove trespassers on land which are clearly directed at "new age travellers", and sections 63 to 67 confer powers directed against the organisers of and participants in raves. The more general powers contained in the new sections 14A–14C of the 1986 Act might be used against, for example, anti-roads protestors or hunt saboteurs. Such persons might also fall foul of the offence of aggravated trespass contained in section 68 of the 1994 Act, which is considered below.

Many assemblies, of course, will not be subject to the rules considered above because they are held indoors. Rallies and meetings are regulated in the first instance by the owner of the property in which they are held, which is often a local authority. Local authorities have statutory duties to make public buildings available for political meetings at election times (Representation of the People Act 1983, ss. 95 and 96). Beyond that, the discretion enjoyed by local authorities over the management of their property, though wide, is not absolute: *Wheeler v. Leicester C.C.* (1985); *R. v. Somerset C.C., ex parte Fewings* (1995). Moreover, local authorities cannot enter into contracts for the hire of a public building for a meeting and then withdraw without payment of damages for breach of contract when it is brought to the authority's attention that the meeting is being held by an unsavoury group: *Verrall v. Great Yarmouth B.C.* (1981).

For completeness, note also that other, non-statutory, controls on assemblies are possible. Interdict may lie to restrain an actual or anticipated demonstration: *McIntyre v. Sheridan* (1993). Those taking part in an assembly may also expose themselves to criminal sanctions (see next section) or civil liability, as in *Thomas v. National Union of Mineworkers* (1985), where Scott J. gave a remedy in damages against picketing miners for nuisance or "unreasonable harassment". The possibility of being convicted of a criminal offence or being faced with liability in damages may well deter people from taking part in legitimate acts of assembly and protest.

PUBLIC ORDER OFFENCES

Watching and besetting

Section 241 of the Trade Union and Labour Relations (Consolidation) Act 1992 provides that a person who "with a view to compel any other person to abstain from doing or to do an act which such other person has a legal right to do or abstain from doing, wrongfully and without legal authority ... watches and besets the house or other place where such other person resides, or works, or carries on business, or happens to be, or the approach to such house or place" shall be guilty of an offence. The offence is especially significant in the context of industrial action, such as picketing, and was used during the miners' strike of 1984–85. It is not confined to picketing or other action outside business premises: in *Galt v. Philp* (1984) participants in a sit-in at a hospital laboratory in Kirkcaldy were convicted of watching and besetting.

Note that the offence requires that action taken is "without legal authority". Section 220 of the Trade Union and Labour Relations (Consolidation) Act 1992 defines lawful picketing as attending, in contemplation or furtherance of an industrial dispute, at or near one's place of work for the purpose only of peacefully obtaining or communicating information, or peacefully persuading any person to work or abstain from working. Picketing which does not fall within this definition, *e.g.* secondary picketing, or primary picketing which is not peaceful, could attract charges of watching and besetting.

Disturbing a meeting

Section 1 of the Public Meeting Act 1908 provides that any person who, at a lawful public meeting, acts in a disorderly manner for the purpose of preventing the transaction of the business for which the meeting was called shall be guilty of an offence.

Disturbing an election meeting

Section 97 of the Representation of the People Act 1983 provides that a person who, at a political meeting held in any constituency between the date of the issue of a writ for the return of an M.P. for that constituency and the date at which a return to the writ is made, acts or incites others to act in a disorderly manner for the purpose of disrupting a meeting shall be guilty of an illegal practice. The same applies to a person who so disrupts a meeting held in relation to a local election in the electoral area for that election on or within three weeks before the date of the election.

Wearing uniforms

Section 1 of the Public Order Act 1936, enacted in response to the rise of fascism in the 1930s, prohibits the wearing of uniforms signifying association with any political organisation or for the promotion of any political object in a public place or at a public meeting. The chief officer of police may, with the consent of the Secretary of State, permit the wearing of a uniform at a "ceremonial, anniversary or other special occasion" if satisfied that this is unlikely to involve any risk of public disorder.

"Uniform" does not require a full, quasi-military outfit. In *R. v. Charnley* (1937) a fascist belt buckle and armband were held to suffice. In *O'Moran v. D.P.P.* (1975) one of the pallbearers at the funeral of an IRA prisoner was convicted under section 1, having attired himself in a black polo-neck jersey, black beret and dark glasses; and in the joined case of *Whelan v. D.P.P.* (1975) the accused was convicted for wearing a black beret at a Sinn Fein rally.

Incitement to racial hatred
Section 17 of the Public Order Act 1986 defines racial hatred as "hatred against a group of persons in Great Britain defined by reference to colour, race, nationality (including citizenship) or ethnic or national origins". The Act creates offences of incitement to racial hatred consisting of the use of words or behaviour or the display of written material (section 18) and of publishing or distributing written material (section 19) which is threatening, abusive and insulting, and which is intended to stir up racial hatred and which is likely, having regard to all the circumstances, to have that effect.

Aggravated trespass
Section 68 of the Criminal Justice and Public Order Act 1994 creates the offence of aggravated trespass. This consists of trespassing on land in the open air with the intention of intimidating persons who are engaging in or about to engage in any lawful activity on that land or adjoining land, so as to deter them from doing so; or with the intention of otherwise obstructing or disrupting that activity. If the senior police officer present at the scene reasonably believes that a person is committing, has committed or intends to commit aggravated trespass, he may direct that person to leave the land. It is an offence to fail to do so or, having left the land, to re-enter it as a trespasser within three months of being directed to leave. It is, however, a defence to prove that one was not trespassing on the land, or that one had a reasonable excuse for failing to leave the land as soon as practicable or for re-entering it.

Obstruction of the highway
In *McAra v. Magistrates of Edinburgh* (1913) Lord Dunedin said that: "The streets are public, but they are public for passage, and there is no such thing as a right in the public to hold meetings as such in the streets. ... [S]treets are for passage, and passage is paramount to everything else."

Section 53 of the Civic Government (Scotland) Act 1982 provides that any person who "being on foot in a public place—(a) obstructs, along with another or others, the lawful passage of any other person and fails to desist on being required to do so by a constable in uniform; or (b) wilfully obstructs the lawful passage of any other person" shall be guilty of an offence. "Obstruct" does not mean to block the street completely. On the contrary, the degree of obstruction necessary to justify arrest and charge is slight. It does not matter that there is some room for passing by, or that only minimal delay for passers-by is caused by the gathering of a crowd.

Obstructing a police officer in the execution of his duty
Section 41 of the Police (Scotland) Act 1967 provides that any person who "assaults, resists, obstructs, molests or hinders a constable in the execution of his duty ... shall be guilty of an offence". In England, the offence may

be committed merely by failing to co-operate with or obey a police officer: *Duncan v. Jones* (1936). In Scotland, at least in the past, it had to be shown that "the obstruction had some physical aspect": *per* Lord Fleming in *Curlett v. McKechnie* (1938). But more recent cases suggest an attenuation of the physical element of the offence. In *Skeen v. Shaw* (1979) it was suggested that "hinders" may not require more than a minimal physical element, even if "assaults" or "obstructs" clearly do.

Mobbing and rioting

The nature of the crime of mobbing and rioting was most recently reviewed by the High Court in *Hancock v. H.M. Advocate* (1981). The elements of the offence are as follows:

- There must be an illegal mob, namely "any assemblage of people, acting together for a common and illegal purpose, effecting or attempting to effect their purpose, either by violence, or by demonstration of force or numbers, or by any species of intimidation, impediment or obstruction calculated to effect their object": *per* Lord Hope in *H.M. Advocate v. Robertson* (1842). How many persons are required to constitute a mob is unclear. In *Sloan v. Macmillan* (1922) counsel submitted that five would be too few; without deciding the point, the court observed that much would depend on "what these people do, the violence they show, the threats they use".
- The mob must have a common criminal purpose. The common purpose need not be formulated in advance: as the Lord Justice-Clerk explained in *Robertson*, "[i]t is enough, that after they [the mob] have been so assembled and brought together, finding their numbers, and ascertaining a common feeling, they then act in concert, and take up and resolve to effect a common purpose". Thus a crowd may assemble peacefully to protest, but if it should then seek to urge its point by violence or intimidation or obstruction, then the crowd becomes a mob and its common purpose unlawful.
- An individual charged with mobbing and rioting must be shown not only to have been present but to have been present in such a way as to "give countenance to the mob" (*H.M. Advocate v. Urquhart* (1844)) and to its common illegal purpose.

Evidential difficulties may arise in proving the third element of the offence. However, in *Winnik v. Allan* (1986) it was held that on a charge of breach of the peace, it may be inferred that the accused "supported and sympathised and encouraged" the crowd's disorderly behaviour by being present in a crowd and failing to dissociate himself from it.

Breach of the peace

The common law offence of breach of the peace, and the police powers which flow from a reasonable apprehension of a breach of the peace, merit a separate section in this chapter.

BREACH OF THE PEACE

The nature of the offence
The police are enjoined by section 17 of the Police (Scotland) Act 1967 to prevent disorder, and are empowered at common law to prevent or restrain breaches of the peace actual or anticipated. This, coupled with the extreme breadth of the offence, confers on the police a wide and flexible power for maintaining public order.

In *Raffaelli v. Heatley* (1949) the Lord Justice-Clerk held that:

"where something is done in breach of public order or decorum which might reasonably be expected to lead to the lieges being alarmed or upset or tempted to make reprisals at their own hand, the circumstances are such as to amount to a breach of the peace."

The offence is not confined to disorderly or aggressive conduct. On the contrary, it was held in *Montgomery v. McLeod* (1977) that:

"There is no limit to the kind of conduct which may give rise to a charge of breach of the peace. All that is required is that there must be some conduct such as to excite the reasonable apprehension to which we have drawn attention [*i.e.* that mischief may ensue] or such as to create alarm and disturbance to the lieges in fact."

But nobody need actually be alarmed or disturbed by the conduct in question, nor need there be an actual danger of mischief ensuing in the form of reprisal in response to the conduct complained of. Lord Dunpark stated clearly in *Wilson v. Brown* (1982) (a case involving high-spirited football fans) that: "Positive evidence of actual harm, upset, annoyance or disturbance created by reprisal is not a prerequisite of conviction."

Thus alarm or disturbance may be treated as a matter of reasonable inference from the circumstances, even if no one was in fact alarmed or disturbed and even if the conduct occurs in private. So in *Wyness v. Lockhart* (1992), the appellants were charged with breach of the peace after approaching two plainclothes police officers, among others, in a street, patting their shoulders and asking for money. Neither the police officers nor anyone else actually approached were alarmed or upset. But, upholding their convictions, the High Court held that the accused's conduct was such as might reasonably be expected to induce alarm, upset or annoyance in members of the public.

In short, it is clear that conduct of a relatively inoffensive kind which as a matter of fact has upset or alarmed nobody may well suffice to found a charge of breach of the peace, provided the conduct was such that upset, alarm or hostile reaction might reasonably be apprehended. More to the point, where the police reasonably anticipate a breach of the peace, they are entitled to intervene to avert it—which may involve uninvited entry into private premises, the imposition of conditions on public meetings, or the dispersal and even outright prevention of public assemblies. Nor are the courts likely to question closely the reasonableness of the views formed by police officers present at the scene (*Ward v. Chief Constable, Strathclyde Police* (1991)).

Power to enter private premises

In *Thomas v. Sawkins* (1935) police officers attended a meeting, anticipating (reasonably) that breaches of the peace might occur. The organiser of the meeting, Mr Thomas, asked the police officers to leave, and when they refused made as if to remove an officer by force. Another officer, P.C. Sawkins, physically restrained Mr Thomas, who then prosecuted P.C. Sawkins for assault. The court held that the police had been lawfully on the premises and that therefore P.C. Sawkins had not assaulted Mr Thomas. Avory J. held that: "the police officers in question had reasonable grounds for believing that, if they were not present, ... a breach of the peace would take place. To prevent ... a breach of the peace, the police were entitled to enter and remain on the premises." More broadly, Lord Hewart C.J. held that: "It is part of the preventative power, and, therefore, part of the preventative duty of the police, in cases where there are ... reasonable grounds of apprehension [of a breach of the peace] to enter and remain on private premises."

In other words, neither express statutory authority nor a warrant is necessary for the police to enter private premises uninvited where a breach of the peace is occurring or is reasonably anticipated.

Power to impose conditions on public meetings

In the Irish case of *Humphries v. Connor* (1864), a police officer requested Mrs Humphries to remove an orange lily from her jacket to prevent a breach of the peace amongst an antagonistic crowd. When she refused, he removed it himself. Mrs Humphries brought an action for assault, but the court, by a majority, accepted the need to prevent a breach of the peace as a good defence.

A step further was taken in *Duncan v. Jones* (1936). Mrs Duncan was preparing to address a crowd outside an unemployment training centre. She had spoken at the same place 14 months before and a disturbance had ensued. To avert the risk of further disturbance, a police officer asked her to move away from the training centre and deliver her speech in a nearby street. She refused, and was charged with and convicted of obstructing a police officer in the execution of his duty. The court observed that once the police officer had formed a reasonable apprehension of a breach of the peace, "it then became his duty to prevent anything which in his view would cause that breach of the peace. While he was taking steps so to do, he was wilfully obstructed by [Mrs Duncan]."

Thirdly, in *Piddington v. Bates* (1961), a police officer attending a trade dispute at a factory took the view that two pickets at each entrance were sufficient, and gave instructions accordingly in order to preserve the peace. Mr Piddington attempted to defy these instructions. He was convicted of obstructing a police officer in the execution of his duty.

These cases illustrate that the police have the power at common law to impose time, place and manner conditions on assemblies independently of their statutory powers under section 14 of the Public Order Act 1986. Nor are these common law powers subject to the limitations contained in section 14: they would apply to assemblies of less than 20 persons, indoors or outdoors. Similarly, a reasonable apprehension of a breach of the peace would seem to involve something less than a risk of "serious public disorder, serious damage to property or serious disruption of the life of the community".

Power to disperse assemblies

The power to order an assembly to disperse, if necessary to prevent a breach of the peace, is but an aspect of the power to impose conditions. Note, however, that a lawful and peaceable assembly as much as a noisy and disorderly one may be ordered to disperse if it is attracting a "hostile audience": it is within the discretion of police officers at the scene to break up the assembly rather than deal with hecklers. Thus in *Deakin v. Milne* (1882), Salvation Army marches in Arbroath had attracted the aggressive opposition, as Salvation Army marches throughout Britain were apt to do at the time, of the so-called Skeleton Army. To preserve the peace, Arbroath magistrates banned Salvation Army marches. The Salvationists defied the ban and were convicted of breaching the ban and of breach of the peace. The validity of the ban and the convictions was affirmed by the High Court. The Lord Justice-Clerk held:

"the assembling of persons, and the behaviour of persons when they so assemble, shall be within the law. But when it leads to a breach of the peace, however good the intentions of the persons may be, the magistrates are entitled to interfere."

Beatty v. Gilbanks (1882) was an English case having similar facts, but which was differently decided. Field J. considered that the Salvation Army marches caused no disturbance of the peace:

"on the contrary ... the disturbance that did take place was caused entirely by the unlawful and unjustifiable interference of the Skeleton Army ... and ... but for the opposition and molestation offered to the Salvationists by these other persons, no disturbance of any kind would have taken place."

Powerful as *Beatty v. Gilbanks* is as an expression of civil liberty, it must be regarded as superseded by the later cases of *Duncan v. Jones* and *Piddington v. Bates*.

Power to prevent assemblies

During the miners' strike of 1984–85, the police power to prevent breaches of the peace was used to stop assemblies forming altogether. In Scotland, the police turned back vehicles carrying miners to prevent them forming mass pickets at Hunterston ore terminal and Ravenscraig steelworks. In England, police road blocks were set up to prevent miners leaving their own counties (such as the Dartford Tunnel roadblock stopping miners from Kent travelling to picket lines on the Nottinghamshire coalfield) and to keep them away from the vicinity of collieries. Attempts to defy police directions were met with arrest and charge, usually for obstructing a police officer in the execution of his duty. A report on the policing of the miners' strike likened these practices to "the Soviet internal passport system or South African pass laws", but their legality was confirmed in *Moss v. McLachlan* (1985). There, four striking miners appealed against their convictions for obstructing a police officer on the basis that he was not acting in the execution of his duty because he had no power to turn them back or to refuse to let them proceed. Skinner J. held:

"Provided [the senior police officers] present honestly and reasonably form the opinion that there is a real risk of a breach of the peace in the sense that it is close proximity both in place and time, then the conditions exist for reasonable preventive acting including, if necessary, the measures taken in this case."

The miners in *Moss* were stopped and arrested one and a half miles from their destination. It is questionable whether, say, the Dartford Tunnel roadblock could, or should, also be held to satisfy the condition of "close proximity both in place and time".

---

11. JUDICIAL REVIEW

THE SCOPE OF JUDICIAL REVIEW

Judicial review invokes the supervisory jurisdiction of the Court of Session, as distinct from its appellate jurisdiction. It is concerned with the legality or validity of the acts and decisions of (primarily) governmental and other public bodies, not with the merits of those acts and decisions. In 1985, a special procedure was introduced to facilitate access to the supervisory jurisdiction (see Rule 58 of the Rules of the Court of Session). The leading modern authority on the scope of the supervisory jurisdiction, and hence of judicial review, is *West v. Secretary of State for Scotland* (1992), where Lord President Hope held that:

"The Court of Session has power, in the exercise of its supervisory jurisdiction, to regulate the process by which decisions are taken by any person or body to whom a jurisdiction, power or authority has been delegated or entrusted by statute, agreement or any other instrument. ... The cases in which the exercise of the supervisory jurisdiction is appropriate involve a tripartite relationship between the person or body to whom the jurisdiction, power or authority has been delegated or entrusted, the person or body by whom it has been delegated or entrusted and the person or persons in respect of or for whose benefit that jurisdiction, power or authority is to be exercised."

This makes clear that review is not confined to the statutory powers of administrative bodies. Prerogative powers are also, in principle, reviewable: *CCSU v. Minister for the Civil Service* (1985). Equally, the supervisory jurisdiction may also extend to the acts and decisions of bodies which are not obviously "public", provided a reviewable jurisdiction exists: *e.g. Forbes v. Underwood* (1886); *St Johnstone F.C. v. Scottish Football Association* (1965); *Bank of Scotland v. Investment Management Regulatory Organisation* (1989).

Note also that just because a body is "public" does not mean that all of its acts and decisions will be subject to review. In *West* itself, it was held that the dispute between Mr West and the Secretary of State was essentially contractual, relating to the terms and conditions of Mr West's employment as a prison officer. It therefore failed Lord Hope's "tripartite relationship" test (see also *Blair v. Lochaber D.C.* (1995)). But in other cases of public employment, *e.g. Rooney v. Chief Constable, Strathclyde Police* (1996) and *Maclean v. Glasgow City Council* (1997), review has been held to be competent even though the petitions involved questions of an individual's contract. It may be that, where the court finds difficulty in applying the "tripartite relationship" test to the facts before it, the test collapses into something akin to the public/private law divide adopted to determine the scope of review in England (for discussion of the difficulties of the tripartism approach, see *Naik v. University of Stirling* (1994) and *Joobeen v. University of Stirling* (1995)). Nevertheless, uncertainties at the edges should not blind you to the fact of certainty at the core.

TITLE AND INTEREST

A petitioner must show title and interest to sue. For an individual to have title: "he must be a party (using the word in its widest sense) to some legal relationship which gives him some right which the person against whom he raises the action either infringes or denies" (*per* Lord Dunedin in *D. & J. Nicol v. Dundee Harbour Trustees* (1915)).

In *D. & J. Nicol*, the pursuers were held to have title to sue as harbour ratepayers—"members of a constituency erected by Act of Parliament ... and ... persons for whose benefit the harbour is kept up". Thus, title may be derived from the statutory relationship created between the parties by Act of Parliament. In the absence of a direct statutory relationship, title to sue may be founded on a statutory function owed to the public as a whole or to a class of the public: *Wilson v. IBA* (1979).

The concept of interest was explained by Lord Ardwell in *Swanson v. Manson* (1907):

"The grounds for this rule are (1) that the law courts of the country are not instituted for the purpose of deciding academic questions of law, but for settling disputes where any of the lieges has a real interest to have a question determined which involves his pecuniary rights or his status; and (2) that no person is entitled to subject another to the trouble and expense of a litigation unless he has some real interest to enforce or protect."

Lord Clyde held in *Scottish Old People's Welfare Council, Petitioners* (1987) that the phrase "pecuniary rights or status" should not be regarded as "an exhaustive or complete description of what may comprise an interest". Nevertheless, in that case, his Lordship held that the petitioners' interest was insufficient to give them a right to sue. The petitioners, a pressure group campaigning on behalf of the elderly, challenged the legality of instructions in a government circular concerning the allocation of cold weather payments to social security claimants. They lacked sufficient interest because they were "not suing as a body of potential claimants but as a body working to protect and advance the interests of the aged".

It is in the public interest that all official decisions should be made lawfully; it is also in the public interest that public bodies should not be exposed to vexatious litigation by busybodies. The approach taken to sufficiency of interest in Scotland, however, does not seem to countenance an active role in the supervision of administrative legality for pressure groups and genuinely concerned, if not directly interested, members of the public (although recent cases may indicate a relaxation in the attitude of the Court of Session to "representative" petitions brought by organisations rather than individuals: *Cockenzie and Port Seton Community Council v. East Lothian D.C.* (1996) and *Educational Institute for Scotland v. Robert Gordon University* (1996)).

GROUNDS FOR JUDICIAL REVIEW

In *CCSU v. Minister for the Civil Service* (1985), Lord Diplock summarised the grounds on which judicial review may be sought:

"Judicial review has I think developed to a stage today when one can conveniently classify under three heads the grounds on which administrative action is subject to control by judicial review. The first ground I would call 'illegality', the second 'irrationality' and the third 'procedural impropriety'."

These three headings—illegality, irrationality and procedural impropriety—are compendious. Each has therefore to be broken down into smaller segments if you are to understand the various grounds on which an administrative act or decision may be challenged. You must also remember that the principles discussed below do not lend themselves to simplistic or rigid analysis: they interact, overlap and are open to future adaptation and extension.

ILLEGALITY

In the most straightforward sense, an act will be illegal or *ultra vires* if it is done without legal authority. Thus in *McColl v. Strathclyde R.C.* (1983) the council was held to have acted *ultra vires* in adding fluoride to the public water supply. The duty laid on the council by the Water (Scotland) Act 1980 was to supply wholesome water. The fluoride was added not to improve the wholesomeness of the water but to improve dental health.

A related situation is where the decision-maker misconstrues the provisions which empower him to act or decide. This may involve an error of the most basic sort, as in *Watt v. Lord Advocate* (1979). There, a National Insurance Commissioner had decided that Mr Watt was subject to a statutory disqualification for receiving unemployment benefit. Striking the decision down, the court held that the Commissioner had not merely misconstrued the statutory provisions relevant to the question of Mr Watt's entitlement to benefits, but had misunderstood the question itself and had proceeded to answer another one. More broadly, a decision may be invalid if it is based on a "material error of law going to the root of the question for determination" (*per* Lord President Emslie, *Wordie Property Co. v. Secretary of State for Scotland* (1984)). As this implies, not every error of law will suffice to invalidate a decision; and, as this implies in turn, it must theoretically be possible to distinguish between errors of law which are sufficiently "material" and those which the decision-maker can make without destroying his authority to decide.

"Material" errors of fact may have similar consequences. Where certain facts are a pre-condition for the exercise of decision-making power, the courts will ascertain that the correct factual basis was indeed established if a decision is challenged on the grounds that it was not: *e.g. R. v. Home Secretary, ex parte Khawaja* (1984).

The constitutional justification for review on jurisdictional grounds is compelling, especially in relation to the review of statutory powers. Parliament confers powers which are limited in terms of the statutory wording. It is not for the donee of such powers to enlarge the scope of the authority that Parliament intended him to have by using his power as the basis for action which was not in fact authorised; or, having misinterpreted the wording of the statute, by using his power on an erroneous basis of law or fact. The role of the courts is to police the boundaries of powers so conferred, in order to ensure that, in accordance with Parliament's intention, the donee remains within the ambit of his authority. But review under the heading of illegality does not end here, and as we move further out, this constitutional justification for review may become somewhat attenuated. Here we are concerned with illegality as *irrelevancy* or *impropriety of purpose* or *bad faith*.

First, the courts see it as implicit in any grant of power that it must be exercised having regard to all relevant considerations and excluding any irrelevant ones. A number of cases involving decisions taken partly in furtherance of political or moral beliefs illustrate the point. In *Gerry Cottle's Circus v. City of Edinburgh D.C.* (1990), the council refused a licence to the circus on the basis of its policy against circuses featuring performing animals. The refusal was held unlawful in that the council had failed to have regard to its statutory duties and powers, and in that this decision was inconsistent with other decisions it had made in the same area. In *Bromley*

LBC v. Greater London Council (1983), the House of Lords held that the GLC had acted illegally in implementing a manifesto pledge of the majority Labour group to reduce fares on public transport in London. This was because the GLC could not use its powers to achieve a social policy which conflicted with statutory obligations to run London transport according to ordinary business principles; and because the fare reduction involved a breach of the council's fiduciary duty to ratepayers. The House of Lords added that the majority group did not possess a mandate to cut fares in the light of their manifesto pledge (although their Lordships' attitude to the relevance of manifesto pledges here might be contrasted with their view on the same point in *Education Secretary v. Tameside MBC* (1977)).

The use of powers to further improper purposes is closely related to the failure to take account of relevant considerations, or the taking into account of irrelevant ones, as a form of illegality. In *Padfield v. Minister of Agriculture* (1968), the House of Lords held that discretion was entrusted to the minister so that he might promote the policy and purposes of the legislation, and that he was not at liberty to thwart those purposes by misinterpreting them. A recent Scottish case on this point is *Highland R.C. v. British Railways Board* (1996). The Railways Act 1993 lays down procedures to be followed if it is proposed to close a line or withdraw services. Having resolved to withdraw the Fort William to London sleeper service, and in an attempt to avoid observance of the closure procedures, British Rail ran "ghost trains" on the line, so that there was, arguably, a "railway passenger service" being provided but one which was not being used. The First Division held this device to be illegal as being outwith the policy and purposes envisaged by Parliament in the legislation.

It is perhaps difficult to conceive of decisions which are flawed for bad faith but which could not be attacked on grounds of irrelevancy or impropriety of purpose. To that extent, bad faith as a ground of review may be somewhat superfluous. But the courts may choose to couch their judgments in terms of bad faith where dishonesty, malice or spite is present. Thus in *Roncarelli v. Duplessis* (1959), Mr Roncarelli's liquor licence was revoked on the direction of the Premier of Québec. The direction was motivated by Mr Roncarelli's repeated provision of bail for fellow Jehovah's Witnesses, who had been charged with offences relating to the distribution of religious literature. Unsurprisingly, the revocation of the licence was struck down.

IRRATIONALITY

This term denotes the courts' substantive control of discretion. The threshold of irrationality necessary to attract judicial intervention is pitched very high. As Lord Greene M.R. explained in *Associated Provincial Picture Houses v. Wednesbury Corporation* (1948):

"It is not what the court considers unreasonable ... . If it is what the court considers unreasonable, the court may very well have different views to that of the local authority on matters of high public policy of this kind. ... The effect of the legislation is not to set the court up as an arbiter of the correctness of one view over another. It is the local authority that are set in that position and, provided they act ... within the four corners of their jurisdiction, this court, in my opinion, cannot interfere."

This expresses the courts' sensitivity to their constitutional position in the context of review. Even review on the grounds of relevancy and propriety of purpose, although it is presented as a technical matter of statutory interpretation, may risk trespassing on the merits of discretionary decisions. In the context of review for irrationality, this danger is inescapably apparent. Therefore, the courts will not intervene unless the decision under attack is "unreasonable in the sense that the court considers it to be a decision that no reasonable body could have come to" (*per* Lord Greene M.R. in *Wednesbury*) or "so outrageous in its defiance of logic or of accepted moral standards that no sensible person who had applied his mind to the question to be decided could have arrived at it" (*per* Lord Diplock in *CCSU v. Minister for the Civil Service* (1985)).

As with bad faith, it is difficult to imagine a decision which passes the tests of relevancy and propriety of purpose but which is, nevertheless, unreasonable in this substantive sense. Yet this does not seem to stop petitioners invoking irrationality as a ground of attack, and even if in most cases the attack fails, there are still several reported cases where it has succeeded. It is arguable that, while the courts insist on the stringency of the *Wednesbury* test, in practice they apply a more relaxed criterion. If so, the greater scope for judicial substitution of judgment is obvious.

Thus in *Kelly v. Monklands D.C.* (1986), it was held that the council's decision that two teenage girls were not "vulnerable" in terms of the Housing (Homeless Persons) Act 1977 was a decision which, in the circumstances, no reasonable authority could have reached. In *James Aitken & Sons v. City of Edinburgh D.C.* (1989), a grant of planning permission was held invalid for irrationality because it was made whilst an earlier application by the same applicants for permission to develop the same site was awaiting decision on appeal to the Secretary of State. No reasonable authority charged with duties under the planning legislation would have acted in this way. Again, in *Woods v. Secretary of State for Scotland* (1991), it was held to be irrational for the respondent to refuse to pay a student's university fees because of the student's alleged failure to meet a deadline for applications, despite the respondent's argument that to make an exception would be unfair to others whose similar cases had been rejected.

Related to irrationality as a ground of review is the principle of proportionality. This requires a decision-maker to have regard to the balance between means and ends: put bluntly, one should not use a sledgehammer to crack a nut. It has not as yet been received into either Scots or English law, although there are cases where the lack of proportion between a decision and the facts upon which it is based has been taken into account, *e.g. R. v. Barnsley MBC, ex parte Hook* (1976). But it may be said that, in these cases, the disproportion was sufficiently severe to amount to *Wednesbury* unreasonableness anyway. An attempt to advance arguments based on proportionality failed in *R. v. Home Secretary, ex parte Brind* (1991). The House of Lords declined to adopt a test of proportionality going beyond that of irrationality as traditionally understood. Lord Ackner and Lord Lowry in particular were concerned that to adopt such a test would inevitably involve "inquiry into and a decision upon the merits". Their Lordships did not, however, rule out the adoption of proportionality at some future date, and developments since *Brind* may indicate some movement in that direction in cases which the courts deem worthy of stricter scrutiny.

PROCEDURAL IMPROPRIETY

In the narrow sense, this head of review may involve no more than failure to comply with prescribed procedural requirements. We might also consider under this heading improper delegation and the unlawful fettering of discretion. More broadly, the courts regard it as implicit in every grant of power that the power will be exercised in accordance with the rules of natural justice: the rule against bias (*nemo judex in sua causa*) and the right to a fair hearing (*audi alteram partem*). From these twin principles, the courts have developed a general duty to act fairly, the content of which varies according to context and circumstances. Increasingly, fairness is held to require that reasons are given for decisions. Similarly, it may be fair to extend procedural protection to legitimate expectations.

Compliance with procedural requirements
Legislation often prescribes specific procedural requirements which the decision-maker should observe in the process of reaching a decision, *e.g.* the giving of notice to third parties, or a requirement of prior consultation. A distinction is often drawn here between mandatory and directory procedural requirements. Broadly speaking, compliance with the former is necessary for the validity of a decision; compliance with the latter is not. Note, however, that the distinction has not met with universal approval. In *London and Clydeside Estates v. Aberdeen D.C.* (1980), Lord Hailsham L.C. regarded the distinction as over-rigid: the problem was one of degree rather than one of category.

Failure to comply with a procedural requirement might amount to a fundamental flaw in the decision-making process. Equally, it might involve nothing more than a trivial defect which the courts would probably ignore. In most cases, the importance of a procedural requirement cannot be determined in the abstract, so that the better approach is to assess on a case-by-case basis how far a failure to comply has caused prejudice to the person concerned.

Improper delegation
As a rule, a power vested in a particular person must be exercised by that person. But this rule is not absolute. Delegation is permissible in certain circumstances, having regard to such factors as the statutory background, the nature of the power which is delegated and the type of person or body to which it is delegated.

Thus it is accepted that where powers are granted to a minister, they can validly be exercised by officials in the minister's department (*Carltona v. Commissioner for Works* (1943)) unless the enabling statute makes clear that the power must be exercised by the minister personally (*Lavender & Son v. Minister for Housing and Local Government* (1970)). In *R. v. Home Secretary, ex parte Oladehinde* (1991) the House of Lords held that the Secretary of State could lawfully delegate his power to deport to immigration officers of sufficient grade and experience, provided that this involved no conflict with the officers' own statutory duties. In general, then, it must be shown that delegation was, expressly or impliedly, within the contemplation of the legislation.

Unlawful fettering of discretion
It is implicit in every grant of discretionary power that the donee of the power remains free to exercise that discretion whenever necessary. He may not bind himself in advance as to the way his discretion might be exercised. Thus, public authorities may not enter into contracts binding them to act in a certain way: *Ayr Harbour Trustees v. Oswald* (1883). Only if the contract is compatible with the authority's statutory duties and powers will it be valid: *R. v. Hammersmith and Fulham LBC, ex parte Beddowes* (1987). Similarly, where a public authority has made representations, it cannot be argued that the authority is unable to resile from the understandings it has created. The doctrine of personal bar does not apply to permit the authority unlawfully to extend the scope of its powers. Thus in *Western Fish Products v. Penwith D.C.* (1981), the company had purchased an industrial site and asserted a user right which would allow it to carry on its business there without the need for planning permission. A letter from a planning officer at the council appeared to accept this, and in reliance on the letter work commenced at the site. Subsequently, the council refused planning permission and served enforcement notices on the company. The Court of Appeal rejected the argument that the planning officer's representation barred the council from refusing planning permission.

It is not only by contract or representation that a public body may unlawfully fetter its discretion. Where a public authority has to make many individual decisions in the same area, consistency of decision-making and administrative efficiency may well demand the adoption of general policies to guide the decision-making process. This is acceptable so long as the policy does not amount to a blanket rule. Policies applied in an over-rigid manner which fails to allow for individuated decisions where necessary will be illegal: *British Oxygen Co. v. Board of Trade* (1971).

Note, however, that assurances, representations or policies may generate legitimate expectations which will be protected by the courts. This is discussed below.

Natural justice: the rule against bias
Self-evidently, cases where an official has a pecuniary or proprietary interest in the outcome of the decision-making process offend against this rule and "attract the full force [of the requirement] that justice must not only be

done but must manifestly be seen to be done" (*per* Lord Goff in *R. v. Gough* (1993)). Beyond that, the test prescribed in *Gough* is whether there is a "real danger" of bias, which denotes a possibility rather than a probability. The range of situations which may give rise to a real danger of bias are legion. Apart from direct financial interest in a decision, other instances giving rise to a perception of unfairness include personal friendship (or personal animosity) between the decision-maker and the subject of the decision; ties of family or professional relationship; or participation by a decision-maker in an appeal against his own decision. This latter situation is not dissimilar to the facts of *Barrs v. British Wool Marketing Board* (1957). Assessors for the Board had valued Mr Barrs' wool at a price with which he disagreed. He appealed to the Board and appeared at a hearing before it along with the assessors. After the hearing, the Board retired to consider its verdict in the company of one of the assessors. The Court of Session reduced the Board's decision to uphold the assessors' valuation for breach of natural justice.

Natural justice: the right to a hearing and the duty to act fairly

Prior to the decision of the House of Lords in *Ridge v. Baldwin* (1964), the courts tended to confine the application of the rules of natural justice to decisions of a judicial or quasi-judicial character. *Ridge* established (or revived) the broader application of natural justice. It was held in that case that a chief constable who was dismissable only for cause was entitled to notice of the charge against him and to an opportunity to be heard in his own defence before he could be lawfully dismissed. But the importance of *Ridge* lies in their Lordships' more general discussion of the principles of natural justice and their disapproval of the constraints on their application imposed by the judicial/administrative dichotomy.

At the same time, however, the House of Lords gave little indication of where the right to a hearing should apply and to what extent. As court proceedings illustrate, the right involves, at its fullest, proceedings in public, notice of proceedings, the opportunity to make representations and lead evidence, cross-examination of witnesses, legal representation, reasons for the decision and the right to an appeal or rehearing. If the principles of natural justice are to obtain in purely administrative situations, it is plain that the application of the right to a hearing, at least, must be qualified if the administrative process is not to be brought to a complete standstill.

In *Re H. K.* (1967), Lord Parker C.J. spoke not in terms of the principles of natural justice but of "fairness" and a "duty to act fairly". Even so, there remained a need for criteria to determine who should benefit from procedural protection and what, in particular situations, such protection should involve. To some extent, the old habits of classification lingered: "judicial" proceedings might still be expected to attract more in the way of procedural protection than "administrative" proceedings (see *Errington v. Wilson* (1995)), and it was held in *Bates v. Hailsham* (1972) that delegated legislative functions did not involve a need for a hearing at all.

Increasingly, however, the courts have adopted an approach based upon the nature of the right or interest (or legitimate expectation) alleged to be affected by the challenged decision. In *McInnes v. Onslow-Fane* (1978), Megarry V.-C. contrasted the positions of the holder of a licence whose licence is revoked; the individual who applies for renewal of a licence shortly to expire; and the initial applicant for a licence. In the first case, the individual is being deprived of a subsisting interest akin to a property right and as such "the right to an unbiased tribunal, the right to notice of the charges and the right to be heard in answer to the charges … are plainly apt". In relation to the second category, Megarry V.-C. held that "the legitimate expectation of a renewal of the licence … is one which raises the question of what it is that has happened to make the applicant unsuitable for the … licence for which he was previously thought suitable". Therefore, he is entitled to a higher degree of procedural protection than the initial applicant, from whom "nothing is being taken away, and in all normal circumstances there are no charges and so no requirement of an opportunity of being heard in answer to the charges".

In summary, there are three basic points to have in mind when considering the application of natural justice or fairness:

- The preliminary question of entitlement is primarily a function of the nature of the petitioner's right or interest and the impact that the challenged decision is alleged to have thereon.
- The content of the duty to act fairly is variable: "the so-called rules of natural justice are not engraved on tablets of stone. … What the requirements of fairness demand … depends on the character of the decision-making body, the kind of decision it has to make, and the statutory or other framework in which it operates" (*per* Lord Bridge in *Lloyd v. McMahon* (1987)).
- The nature of and impact upon the petitioner's rights or interests is not the only relevant factor in determining the content of the duty to act fairly. Certainly where statutory powers are concerned, the statutory background is important, and where a statute lays down detailed and precise procedures to be followed, the courts are likely to regard that as final: *Wiseman v. Borneman* (1971).

Fairness and legitimate expectations

The duty to act fairly applies not only where harm to an individual's legal rights or interests is in issue. In *Schmidt v. Home Secretary* (1967), two American Scientology students had been admitted to the United Kingdom for a limited period. On the expiry of that period, the Home Secretary refused them an extension of leave to remain. The students challenged this decision on the grounds, *inter alia*, that it was made without a hearing. The Court of Appeal dismissed the action, but Lord Denning M.R. observed:

"The speeches in *Ridge* v *Baldwin* show that an administrative body may, in a proper case, be bound to give a person who is affected by their decision an opportunity of making representations. It all depends on whether he has some right or interest or, I would add, some legitimate expectation, of which it would not be fair to deprive him without hearing what he has to say."

So, had the applicants' permits been revoked before they expired, they should have been able to make representations because they would have had a legitimate expectation of being allowed to stay in the United Kingdom for the permitted time. But they had neither a right nor a legitimate expectation of being allowed to stay for a longer period, and so an extension of time could be refused without reasons and without a hearing.

The underlying principle here is that legitimate expectations induced by governmental conduct should not be thwarted by behaviour on the part of government which is unpredictable, irregular or arbitrary. It remains difficult, however, accurately to predict when an expectation will be regarded as legitimate. Equally, the nature and scope of the protection derived from a legitimate expectation remains the subject of some controversy.

A legitimate expectation may be derived, in the first place, from an express promise or representation. In *Att.-Gen. of Hong Kong v. Ng Yuen Shiu* (1983), the Hong Kong authorities had announced that illegal immigrants would be interviewed, with each case being dealt with on its merits, before any decision was taken to expel them from the territory. The applicant had entered Hong Kong illegally some years previously, and in the meantime had established a flourishing business. The authorities purported to expel him without an interview. The Privy Council held that, although the duty to act fairly might not generally apply to illegal immigrants, the Hong Kong authorities had by their assurances created a legitimate expectation of a hearing which should be enforced.

Secondly, a legitimate expectation may be derived from an implied representation based upon the past practice of the decision-maker. A representation, whether express or implied, must be "clear, unambiguous and devoid of relevant qualification" (*per* Bingham L.J. in *R. v. Inland Revenue Commissioners, ex parte MFK Underwriting Agencies* (1990)). Thus in *CCSU v. Minister for the Civil Service* (1985), the established practice of consultation with staff unions at GCHQ before making changes in the terms and conditions of their service was held to generate a legitimate expectation of consultation (but see below). Similarly, in *R. v. Home Secretary, ex parte Khan* (1985), the Home Office issued a circular stating the criteria which the Home Secretary would apply in cases of international adoption. Relying on these criteria, the applicant sought entry clearance for his nephew from Pakistan; on the basis of different criteria, clearance was refused. Parker L.J. held that the Home Secretary could not depart from his stated policy "without affording interested persons a hearing and only then if the overriding public interest demands it."

This reference to the "public interest" serves to emphasise that the individual's legitimate expectation may be outweighed by competing considerations. Again, *CCSU* provides an example: the unions' legitimate expectation of consultation on the proposed ban on union membership was held to be overridden by the public interest in national security, which the minister claimed was threatened by industrial action at GCHQ. In general terms, it is obviously important that, notwithstanding the creation of legitimate expectations, public bodies should be able to alter their policies and practices as the public interest requires. But the doctrine of legitimate expectations serves to remind government that, in so doing, it must, in fairness, treat individuals' legitimate expectations with the degree of respect that is compatible with the wider public interest.

It is now settled that legitimate expectations may attract procedural protection. But does the concept also embrace *substantive* protection of the interest, benefit or advantage itself? Most recent authority suggests that it does not. In *R. v. Home Secretary, ex parte Hargreaves* (1997), Pill L.J. held:

"I cannot agree … that the court can take and act upon an overall view of the fairness of the respondent's decision in substance. The court can quash the decision only if, in relation to the expectation and in all the circumstances, the decision to apply the new policy in the particular case was unreasonable in the *Wednesbury* sense. The claim to a broader power to judge the fairness of a decision in substance … is in my view wrong in principle."

There are relatively few instances of the concept of legitimate expectation being applied in Scotland. One of the more prominent is *Walsh v. Secretary of State for Scotland* (1990). Mr Walsh was serving a prison sentence in Scotland, where remission is one half of the sentence. The Court of Session held that he had a legitimate expectation, when he was transferred to a prison in England, where remission is one third of the sentence, that the earlier release date would apply. More recently, in *Rooney v. Chief Constable, Strathclyde Police* (1996), the petitioner, a former police constable, sought judicial review of the chief constable's refusal to accept the withdrawal of his resignation on the grounds that he had a legitimate expectation that the chief constable would adhere to published procedures. Lady Cosgrove agreed that such an expectation was legitimate, but held that it did not extend to an expectation of a right to withdraw resignation once given.

Fairness and the duty to give reasons
It is still often said that there is no general duty at common law to give reasons for decisions: *R. v. Higher Education Funding Council, ex parte Institute of Dental Surgery* (1994). However, the exceptions that have been made to that general principle may suggest that the sum of the exceptions is now greater than the principle itself.

It was held in *Padfield v. Minister of Agriculture* (1968) that the courts might require reasons where necessary to rebut an inference of irrationality. This was one of the grounds for the Court of Appeal decision in *R. v. Civil Service Appeal Board, ex parte Cunningham* (1991), where a prison officer who had been unfairly dismissed challenged the Board's decision to award him only £6,500 in circumstances where an industrial tribunal would have awarded two or three times as much. More broadly, however, the Court of Appeal also held that in the circumstances, reasons were required as a matter of fairness. The House of Lords followed this broader approach in *R. v. Home Secretary, ex parte Doody* (1994), which concerned the right of prisoners given mandatory life sentences to know the reasons for the determination of the "tariff" element of their sentences. Their Lordships held that the Home Secretary was under a duty to give reasons here both because fairness required it and because the absence of reasons, by making the detection of errors impossible, frustrated the prisoners' right to seek judicial review of the Home Secretary's decisions.

Where reasons are required, they must be adequate. Thus in *Zia v. Home Secretary* (1994), Lord Prosser reduced an immigration adjudicator's refusal of entry clearance on the grounds that the written reasons were unclear and insufficient. In *Safeway Stores v. National Appeal Panel* (1996) it was held that the reasoning given in support of the Panel's decision was inadequate in that it merely paraphrased the applicable regulations without indicating what the real reasons and material considerations were.

APPENDIX: SAMPLE EXAMINATION QUESTIONS AND ANSWER PLANS

1. IS THE IDEA OF INDIVIDUAL MINISTERIAL RESPONSIBILITY NO MORE THAN NOSTALGIA FOR THE PAST?

Note first that the title directs you to individual ministerial responsibility. Do not therefore embark on a lengthy discussion of collective ministerial responsibility: however correct you may be, you will get no credit for it. Your essay might be structured as follows:

Outline of the traditional convention of individual ministerial responsibility

Based on nineteenth century practice: ministers were expected to know about the workings of their departments and submit to the scrutiny of Parliament about their own and their civil servants' conduct of departmental affairs. The minister took the credit for success; he also bore sole responsibility for failure. If Parliament was dissatisfied with the minister, it might withdraw its confidence from him on a motion of censure, obliging him to resign (which he might prefer to do voluntarily). Thus Parliament could enforce the convention.

Twentieth century practice

Very few post-war examples of ministerial resignations in accordance with the convention (but note, *e.g.* Dugdale in 1954; Carrington in 1982). Party lines are more rigid and party discipline stricter, enabling a government with a Commons majority to protect a minister from a motion of censure. Parliament's ability to enforce ministerial responsibility has thus been weakened. Also, government today is much larger and more complex. Is it then realistic or fair to expect a minister to know everything that is done or not done in his department, and to expect him to resign even for errors of his civil servants about which he knew nothing? A distinction has been drawn between "responsibility" in the sense of "liability to resign" and "accountability" meaning the minister's theoretically unimpaired duty to give a full and frank account to Parliament of the deeds and misdeeds of his department (and of the agencies and contractors to which, in modern times, administration is often delegated); see, *e.g.* the Maxwell-Fyfe guidelines of 1954. This may be a sensible distinction to draw in modern circumstances: provided ministers do submit in good faith to parliamentary scrutiny, it should not matter whether resignations occur for departmental mistakes. But if there is no sanction, can ministers be forced to honour their obligation to account to Parliament? Is there evidence to suggest that ministers do not in fact honour this obligation to explain and justify departmental acts and decisions? If ministers cannot be forced either to resign or to account, does that not leave the idea of individual ministerial responsibility as "nostalgia for the past"?

Assessment
There is evidence to suggest that ministerial responsibility to Parliament in its current form is inadequate as a mechanism of accountability; see, *e.g.* the Scott Report (1996). But the *idea* of ministerial responsibility cannot be regarded as "nostalgia for the past": on the contrary, the responsibility of the executive to Parliament is a constitutional fundamental. There may be shortcomings in the practical operation of ministerial responsibility to Parliament in modern practice, but that does not invalidate the idea. We should perhaps seek to reanimate the idea by finding ways of redressing the imbalance of power between government and Parliament, thus enabling M.P.s to hold the government to account more effectively than existing devices such as Parliamentary Questions and debates permit (*e.g.* by providing select committees with powers to order disclosure of government information).

2. "ULTIMATELY, NOTHING IN THE EUROPEAN COMMUNITIES ACT 1972 ABRIDGES PARLIAMENTARY SUPREMACY." DISCUSS.

Since the title directs you to the effects of the European Communities Act 1972, you should not spend time discussing other lines of attack on the doctrine of parliamentary supremacy. You may accept for the purposes of the essay that the doctrine is correct. The question is whether it must now be qualified in view of United Kingdom membership of the European Union. You might structure your essay as follows:

The nature of parliamentary supremacy
Point out that, as Dicey defined it, parliamentary supremacy means, first, that Parliament can make or unmake any law whatever; and, secondly, that no court or other body may question or set aside an Act of Parliament.

Support for the doctrine is to be found both in statutes and case law. By ordinary statute, Parliament has legislated extra-territorially and retrospectively; it has amended or repealed "fundamental" provisions of the Union legislation; and it has enacted legislation of great constitutional importance. Case law indicates that courts in the United Kingdom recognise later statutes as "impliedly repealing" earlier ones (so that Parliament's continuing sovereignty is unimpaired), *e.g. Ellen Street Estates v. Minister of Health* (1934); and decline in any case to question the validity of statutes, *e.g. Pickin v. British Railways Board* (1974).

You should also highlight the two basic points about Dicey's doctrine: first, it holds that Parliament has unlimited legislative competence in a legal sense; it does not suggest that Parliament is free from practical or political constraints; secondly, it expresses the relationship between Parliament and the courts, and the effect to be given by the courts to Acts of Parliament.

Community law

Note first that well before the United Kingdom joined the European Communities in January 1973, the primacy of E.C. law over the national law of member states was well-established in the jurisprudence of the ECJ. Since membership involved a "permanent limitation on their sovereign rights", member states could not legally enact legislation incompatible with E.C. law: *Costa v. ENEL* (1964). European Community law prevails even over conflicting provisions of national constitutions: *Internationale Handelsgesellschaft* (1970). The ECJ also made clear, albeit after the United Kingdom became a member state, that national courts themselves were bound to "disapply" incompatible national law, "whether prior or subsequent to the Community rule": *Simmenthal* (1978). These principles pose an obvious challenge to parliamentary supremacy.

On acceding to the Community treaties, the United Kingdom was obliged to incorporate E.C. law and enable United Kingdom institutions to fulfil the further obligations of membership. The European Communities Act 1972 was enacted to achieve this. You should note section 2(1), which provides for the automatic incorporation of present and future Community rules creating "enforceable rights, powers, liabilities, obligations and restrictions"; section 2(4), which provides that any enactment of the United Kingdom Parliament "passed or to be passed" is to be construed and have effect subject to section 2(1); and section 3, which provides that in all legal proceedings in the United Kingdom, the meaning or effect of E.C. law is to be determined in accordance with the jurisprudence of the ECJ.

United Kingdom courts and E.C. law

Have United Kingdom courts accepted the primacy of E.C. law since the enactment of the 1972 Act? Note, *e.g. Macarthys v. Smith* (1979): Lord Denning M.R. held that E.C. law took precedence over the Equal Pay Act 1970. But that statute was enacted before the European Communities Act; the latter (and thus E.C. law) could be said to have "impliedly repealed" the former. Does E.C. law also take precedence over a subsequent Act of Parliament (as E.C. law requires that it should)? We now know that it does:

R. v. Transport Secretary, ex parte Factortame (No. 2) (1991); *R. v. Employment Secretary, ex parte Equal Opportunities Commission* (1995). These cases tell us that whether an Act of Parliament is passed before or after the relevant Community rule, the United Kingdom courts will presume that any incompatibility was unintended; and that the courts have jurisdiction to declare such incompatibility where it exists.

Does this *ultimately* affect parliamentary supremacy?
It could be argued that, because it required an Act of Parliament to confer primacy within the United Kingdom on E.C. law, an Act of Parliament could take that primacy away. Note that, first, *Factortame* and *EOC* prove that Parliament cannot *impliedly* repeal E.C. law, even if it can do so expressly; secondly, the relationship between Parliament and the courts in the United Kingdom *has* been altered, at least for the time being. We may say now: "Parliament may make or unmake any law whatever and no court is competent to question an Act of Parliament, except where E.C. law applies in which case E.C. law prevails and the courts have jurisdiction to declare an Act of Parliament to be incompatible with E.C. law."

Which leaves the *ultimate* question. Could Parliament *expressly* repeal the European Communities Act, thereby depriving E.C. law of its primacy in the United Kingdom? Views on this differ. Some would say that, were Parliament to do this, United Kingdom courts would obey this latest expression of the sovereign will of Parliament. Others argue that the courts would still be required to "disapply" such a statute, unless and until the United Kingdom negotiates for release from membership and restoration of the sovereignty it transferred to the Community on accession. If you take the latter view, you would have to disagree with the title quotation. We cannot know the answer to this question until the situation actually arises for judicial consideration, but it is arguable that the longer the United Kingdom remains a member state, the more likely it is that United Kingdom courts will hold that, even in the ultimate sense, parliamentary supremacy *has* been abridged.

3. PUBLIC ORDER PROBLEM

The Political Correctness Association (PCA) plans to hold a march from Charlotte Square in Edinburgh, along George Street to the Assembly Rooms, where a public meeting is to be held. Three days before the march, the Unfettered Freedoms Organisation (UFO) hear of it and decide to march from St Andrews Square at the other end of George Street to register their opposition to the aims of the PCA. On the day, Inspector Brown is rather taken aback by the large UFO presence in St Andrews Square. He tells Gregory, convenor of the UFO, to tell his members to stay where they are until the PCA are safely inside the Assembly Rooms. Gregory agrees, but unfortunately the UFO supporters are raring to go.

As the two marches approach one another, the UFO begins to chant "why aren't you at home, girls?" (although the PCA is not exclusively female) and placards bearing quotations from *Viz* magazine are displayed.

Sophie, a PCA member, is so incensed that she runs across to a UFO supporter and tears his placard from him. P.C. White steps in and says "no need for that, darling". Sophie shouts that she won't be spoken to in such a patronising manner and throws the placard at P.C. White.

Taking the view that things are getting out of hand, Inspector Brown tells Gregory that the UFO march is to return to St Andrews Square to allow the PCA to file into the Assembly Rooms. Gregory communicates this order to his members, but a substantial number of them refuse to go back on the grounds of unfettered freedoms. Some, including Gregory, are arrested and charged under the Public Order Act 1986.

Other UFO members manage, by devious means, to get into the PCA meeting and begin to heckle the speakers. Provoked beyond endurance, PCA members argue back in no uncertain terms. Hearing the racket from outside, Inspector Brown and other police officers enter and request Moira, President of the PCA, to tell her members to leave the building and disperse in an orderly fashion. Moira tells Inspector Brown he is "right out of order" and refuses.

Advise the parties

In answering a problem question, you should state the law as it would apply to the facts given. Do not waste time discussing the merits or demerits of the law; no credit will be given.

The legal background

Both the PCA march and the UFO march should have been notified at least seven days in advance to the local authority and the chief constable: Civic Government (Scotland) Act 1982, s. 62. The UFO march cannot have complied with this requirement, although the local authority may waive the requirement of *seven days'* advance notice (if not advance notice as such). Under section 65, it is an offence to hold a procession without giving advance notice, and to take part in such a procession when required to desist by a uniformed police officer.

Whether or not the UFO and its members are in breach of these provisions, Inspector Brown (provided he is the senior police officer present at the scene) has the authority to impose conditions on a march when it is taking place or when people are assembling with a view to taking part in it: Public Order Act 1986, s. 12. Inspector Brown is entitled to request Gregory to keep the UFO in St Andrews Square until the PCA are inside the Assembly Rooms provided that he *reasonably* believes this is necessary to prevent *serious* public disorder, damage to property or disruption of the life of the community; or to prevent intimidation of others with a view to stopping them doing what they have a right to do. But note, *e.g. Ward v. Chief Constable, Strathclyde Police* (1991): only if Inspector Brown formed such a belief in circumstances where no reasonable police officer would have done so will the courts call it into question. Assuming that Inspector Brown acted within his powers under s. 12, those UFO members who *knowingly* failed to comply with the direction to remain in St Andrews Square committed an offence: section 12(4) and (5) (although it is a defence to show that one's failure to comply arose from circumstances beyond one's control).

Sophie
Sophie's actions may render her liable to a charge under section 41 of the Police (Scotland) Act 1967: "assault[ing] ... a police officer in the execution of his duty". If a physical element is still required for this offence (see *Curlett v. McKechnie* (1938)), this would seem to be satisfied. Was P.C. White acting in the execution of his duty? The answer to this must be "yes": police officers have a duty under section 17 of the Police (Scotland) Act 1967 to prevent disorder, and a power at common law to prevent actual or anticipated breaches of the peace. Sophie could also be charged with breach of the peace in that her actions "might reasonably be expected to lead to the lieges being ... tempted to make reprisals": *Raffaelli v. Heatley* (1949). But by the same token, UFO members who took part in the provocative chanting and placard-waving could also be liable to charges of breach of the peace, as could those who were merely present if their presence could be held to have "supported and sympathised and encouraged" the rest: *Winnik v. Allan* (1986).

Gregory
Gregory is arrested and charged under the Public Order Act 1986 when UFO members fail to retreat to St Andrews Square on Inspector Brown's second direction. This must be a charge under section 12(4) of the 1986 Act (we saw before that Gregory and other UFO members might also be charged under section 12(4) and (5) for failure to comply with Inspector Brown's first direction). An initial question is whether Gregory was lawfully arrested. Provided Inspector Brown was acting within his powers under section 12(1) in imposing the condition, and provided the arresting officer made clear to Gregory that he was under legal compulsion and told him the correct reason for his arrest (in accordance with *Forbes v. H.M. Advocate* (1990)), Gregory's arrest will have been lawful. We have seen that the courts are unlikely to question Inspector Brown's belief that the condition he imposed was necessary to prevent serious disorder, damage to property or disruption in the life of the community unless it was a belief no reasonable officer could have formed: *Ward*. A second question is whether Gregory would have a good defence to a charge under section 12(4). Gregory may well be able to show that, in the circumstances, his failure to comply with Inspector Brown's direction did arise from circumstances beyond his control: he did, after all, agree to communicate the direction to UFO members.

Other arrested UFO members
Again, it is likely that the arrest and charge of these people for committing offences under section 12(5) of the Public Order Act 1986 was competent for the reasons discussed in relation to Gregory. They may also be liable to charges of breach of the peace: *Raffaelli v. Heatley* (1949); *Montgomery v. McLeod* (1977). The UFO members who manage by devious means to get into the Assembly Rooms could also be charged with breach of the peace, and also, possibly, the offence contained in section 1 of the Public Meeting

Act 1908: acting, at a lawful public meeting, in a disorderly manner for the purpose of preventing the transaction of the business for which the meeting was called together.

Moira

Moira refuses to comply with Inspector Brown's instructions in the Assembly Rooms. It is clear that Inspector Brown is not acting pursuant to statutory powers here: section 14 of the Public Order Act 1986 gives the police powers to control public assemblies but only if, *inter alia*, they are held in a public place which is wholly or partly open to the air. However, the police have power to enter private premises uninvited if necessary to prevent breaches of the peace which are taking place or which are reasonably apprehended: *Thomas v. Sawkins* (1935). This would seem to justify the police presence in the Assembly Rooms here, on the assumption that the Assembly Rooms are "private premises". Moreover, the police have power to break up assemblies and order them to disperse if necessary to prevent breaches of the peace: *Deakin v. Milne* (1882); *Duncan v. Jones* (1936). Moira could be liable to a charge of breach of the peace (along with others present) if her conduct is such as to excite reasonable apprehension that mischief may ensue or is such as to cause alarm or disturbance to the lieges in fact, bearing in mind that "positive evidence of actual harm, upset, annoyance or disturbance created by reprisal is not a prerequisite of conviction": *Wilson v. Brown* (1982) . She may also be liable to a charge under section 41 of the Police (Scotland) Act 1967, which includes "hindering" a constable in the execution of his duty (on the "execution of duty" point, see the points discussed in relation to Sophie). It was suggested in *Skeen v. Shaw* (1979) that "hinders" in section 41 may not require an element of *physical* obstruction, even if "assaults" does.

4. JUDICIAL REVIEW PROBLEM

A local authority has a discretion under the (imaginary) Community Development Act 1994 to award annual child care grants to anyone undergoing a course of further education. For the past three years, the council has had a well-publicised policy of giving priority to applications from single mothers. The council has now decided not to continue with this policy. It is experiencing severe difficulties in meeting needs in other spending areas. Also, much adverse publicity has been directed at the council in recent months by the local press, attacking "special handouts for feckless gymslip mums".

A local self-help group, Single Mothers Hotline (SMH), has received dozens of calls from anxious parents and is furious that the council has reversed its policy. In the past, SMH has been invited to discuss various policy initiatives relating to one-parent families with the council, and considers that at the very least it ought to have been consulted on this occasion. SMH also has evidence to suggest that not only has priority been withdrawn from single mothers but that the council is no longer making any grants towards child care to help those in further education.

Amanda is about to start the fourth year of her law degree and has been offered a job as a trainee solicitor. For her first three years, she had the benefit of a child care grant which enabled her to place her three-year-old twins in a day nursery. This year her application has been rejected. Amanda is upset about this because she feels that the application form did not give her any opportunity to explain the facts of her situation, and because no reasons were given for the refusal. She has had to take up part time work in a shop and has fallen behind with her studies, and she fears that she will be forced to drop out of her course.

Advise Single Mothers Hotline and Amanda.

Single Mothers Hotline

(a) Title and interest
Would a "local self-help group" have title and interest to seek judicial review of the council's exercise of its discretionary power to award child care grants to those in further education? Where statutory powers are owed to the public, any member of the public (or a body of them) will have title to sue to enforce it: *Wilson v. IBA* (1979). But such title must be qualified by sufficient interest. In *Scottish Old People's Welfare Council, Petitioners* (1987), the petitioners lacked sufficient interest because they were "not suing as a body of potential claimants but as a body working to protect and advance the interests of the aged". What of recent cases more favourable to "representative standing"? In *Educational Institute for Scotland v. Robert Gordon University* (1996), Lord Milligan held that:

"Where ... a trade union is able to allege that amongst its membership are persons who are likely to be adversely affected by an *ultra vires* decision of the respondents and that it is unrealistic for such members individually ... to challenge the decision ... it seems to me that that trade union has ... an interest to challenge the decision."

Could this dictum be extended, by analogy, to SMH?

(b) Illegality
Assuming SMH has title and interest, on what grounds might it seek review? The council's power to award child care grants is discretionary—it may be within the scope of the council's discretion to decide to make no awards in any given year. Note, however, that there is no such thing as "unfettered discretion": *Padfield v. Minister of Agriculture* (1968). The courts presume that all statutory powers are granted for a purpose, so that the council is at least obliged to give due consideration to the exercise of its powers: failure to do so is by definition *ultra vires*. Equally, if it can be shown that the decision here was taken to "penalise" single mothers ("feckless gymslip mums") that would surely be using the statutory discretion for an improper purpose: *Gerry Cottle's Circus v. City of Edinburgh D.C.* (1990).

The council must also exercise its discretion without regard to irrelevant considerations. The fact that the council's former policy was subject to criticism in the press should be irrelevant (see by analogy *R. v. Home Secretary, ex parte Venables* (1997): here, the two boys convicted of the murder of Jamie Bulger sought judicial review of the Home Secretary's decision—taken partly in response to public outcry—to raise the "tariff" period of their sentences from 10 years to 15; the House of Lords quashed the decision, citing the public mood as an irrelevant consideration in the exercise of the Home Secretary's powers). But the courts are unlikely to reduce a decision as irrelevant if it is supportable on other, relevant grounds. The question of resource allocation is clearly a relevant consideration, and the courts might not question too closely the priorities arrived at by a public body operating on a limited budget: *R. v. Environment Secretary, ex parte Hammersmith and Fulham LBC* (1991). Also, it is arguable that if this is a decision the council has reached, the courts should be wary of second-guessing the democratic process: *R. v. Environment Secretary, ex parte Nottinghamshire C.C.* (1986).

(c) Procedural impropriety

First, although the council may adopt policies to guide the way in which it exercises its powers, it may not improperly fetter its discretion by adopting an over-rigid policy—flexibility to deal with individual cases must remain: *British Oxygen Co. v. Board of Trade* (1971). If SMH are correct in thinking that the council has not only discontinued its policy of prioritising single mothers, but has in fact resolved to make no further child care grants, it could argue that the decision was invalid on this ground.

Secondly, it seems that SMH have in the past been invited to discuss policy initiatives relating to one-parent families. We cannot tell whether this denotes an established and consistent practice of consultation, but it is worth noting that SMH may have had a legitimate expectation of consultation here: *CCSU v. Minister for the Civil Service* (1985). If so, failure to consult could render the council's decision invalid for procedural impropriety.

Amanda

(a) Title and interest

Clearly, Amanda as a directly affected person would have title and interest to sue. Also, if she raised a petition for judicial review, the points made in relation to illegality, above, would equally constitute grounds for review here.

(b) Procedural impropriety

The council is under a duty to act fairly; but what does fairness require here? As a first point, what sort of applicant is Amanda? In *McInnes v. Onslow-Fane* (1978) it was held that the applicant for *renewal* of an interest is entitled to more by way of fairness than an initial applicant, including the chance to make representations to the decision-maker. Such an opportunity does not seem to have been extended to Amanda here.

The case law is clear that public bodies must remain free to change their policies as circumstances may require. Even so, the adoption of a policy may generate legitimate expectations which may not be unfairly frustrated unless the overriding public interest requires this: *R. v. Home Secretary, ex parte Khan* (1985); *CCSU*. Thus Amanda could argue that the council cannot, in fairness, lawfully resile from its policy, leaving her high and dry, without first hearing what she has to say. Be careful not to argue that Amanda had a legitimate expectation of being awarded a grant for her fourth year of study: that would be to use the doctrine of legitimate expectation in a substantive way (meaning that in fairness Amanda should get a grant). It was held in *R. v. Home Secretary, ex parte Hargreaves* (1997) that legitimate expectations cannot have such substantive effect.

Is the council's refusal of a grant unlawful for want of reasons? There is no general common law duty to give reasons, but reasons may be required to rebut an inference of irrationality (*Padfield*) or simply as a matter of fairness: *R. v. Home Secretary, ex parte Doody* (1994). Note, however, that in the leading cases on the duty to give reasons, important rights or interests were at stake: personal liberty (*Doody*); loss of livelihood (*R. v. Civil Service Appeal Board, ex parte Cunningham* (1991)). Is Amanda's interest in receiving a benefit on a par with these?

(c) Irrationality

One might draw a parallel between Amanda's case and that of the petitioner in *Kelly v. Monklands D.C.* (1986). But at issue in *Kelly* was the council's statutory *duty* to provide accommodation to the involuntarily homeless. The council determined that Miss Kelly was voluntarily homeless and was not vulnerable; the Court of Session reduced that determination as *Wednesbury* unreasonable. At issue here, however, is a *discretionary power*. Can it be said that the council's decision is irrational in the same way as the decision in *Kelly*?

Amanda might also seek to apply the analogy of *James Aitken & Sons v. City of Edinburgh D.C.* (1989), where the Lord Ordinary reduced the council's decision for irrationality because it had arrived at its decision knowing that it was not in possession of all material facts. Bear in mind that one of Amanda's grievances is the fact that she was not given an opportunity to explain the facts of her situation to the council.

A final point: if it could be argued that, in the circumstances, the decision to refuse Amanda a grant was *prima facie* irrational, reasons might be required to rebut the inference of irrationality: *Padfield v. Minister of Agriculture* (1968).

INDEX